JACOBOWSKY

AND THE

COLONEL

Plays by S. N. Behrman

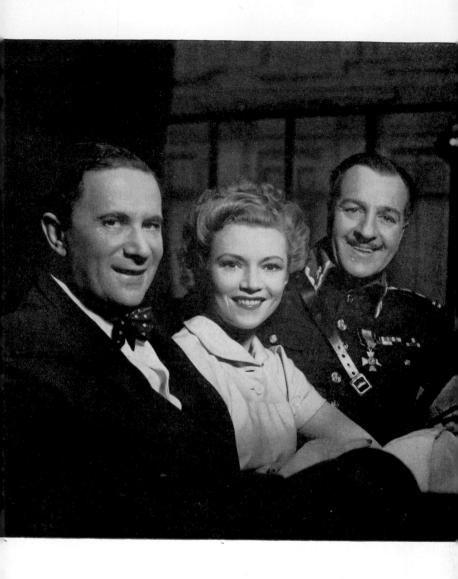

Jacobowsky and the Colonel

Original Play by Franz Werfel

American Play based on same by

S. N. Behrman

RANDOM HOUSE · NEW YORK

FIRST PRINTING

The photographs in this book are by Vandamm Studio

COPYRIGHT, 1944, BY S. N. BEHRMAN

Published simultaneously in Canada by
Random House of Canada Limited

MANUFACTURED IN THE UNITED STATES OF AMERICA

For

ELIA KAZAN

FOREWORD

In Hollywood one evening in the spring of 1941 I was invited
to dinner by the late Max Reinhardt to meet Franz Werfel.
Some months earlier I had read in the New York *Times* an
item to the effect that Mr. Werfel had been captured by the
Nazis in France and killed. His publisher, Mr. Huebsch, told
me that all efforts to reach Werfel, even through the Red Cross,
had been unavailing. Although he had tried through every con-
ceivable agency, he could find out nothing about him, and there
was nothing further he could do.

Here, at Max Reinhardt's dinner table, was the escaped victim,
cherubic, forcing himself to talk, out of courteous deference to
me, an ersatz English, and recounting the long story of his
exaggerated death. I had met many refugees, great and small,
and from all of them I had heard accounts of their experiences.
But this was something new in horror stories. For Mr. Werfel,
talking with a gusto unhalted by the idiosyncrasies of English
syntax, his blue eyes gleaming, kept the table amused and spellbound for well over an hour.

I have never heard or read so vivid an account of what it
meant to be in France in that summer after her fall, a step ahead
of the Nazis: the frantic crowds in front of the consulates, the
pulverization of the consciousness into one acrid grain of desire—
to get a stamp on a piece of paper.

Among the anecdotes Werfel told was one which became fixed
in my mind because of some peculiarity of compactness. A Polish-
Jewish business man buys a car from a rascally chauffeur. Having
bought it, he is faced by his inability to drive it. A reactionary
Polish colonel who can drive happens along.

The colonel consents to drive the car to the coast, first throwing out the refugee's possessions, substituting his own. This seized me at once. There came irresistibly into my mind the pattern of one of my favorite plays, *The Front Page,* by Ben Hecht and Charles MacArthur.

Werfel went on weaving his farcical phantasmagoria—for when the conventions of property, justice, the divisions of life and death are all held in abeyance by an arbitrary god, the habits based on these conventions evidently jumble into farce like a macabre *Alice in Wonderland*—while I kept thinking: "Two men in an ambivalent relationship—two men from the opposite ends of the earth—opposites spiritually, physically, mentally—held together during a flight by a common enemy and a mechanical thing. . . . They hate each other—they part—they miss each other. . . ."

After dinner I went to Werfel in the living room. I told him that I thought that in this story of the Polish refugee and the colonel there might be a comedy. It seemed simple and natural; it seemed to fall out into beautiful folds like a fine linen sheet when you shake it a bit. We stood around there in Max Reinhardt's drawing room shaking it around a bit. It is curious that, in spite of the creative trek this play has taken in the intervening three years, its main outline is the same that it assumed that evening not ten minutes after Werfel had finished his tragicomic odyssey.

How is it that one of the greatest tragedies in history should seem funny on the lips of one who had acutely suffered it? To answer this, one would, perhaps, have to command an ultimate psychology. Why, in exile, do Ernst Toller and Stefan Zweig kill themselves, while Franz Werfel settles down in the same exile to write *Embezzled Heaven* and *The Song of Bernadette*? Why does Virginia Woolf throw herself into a lake, while the speeches of Winston Churchill twinkle with an ineluctable humor? They all saw the same sights, endured the same privations, were faced with the identical dragon. Is humor the amalgam of resilience in adversity? And yet many of the saints and martyrs lacked humor, whatever else they possessed. Perhaps humor is the salt of survival and the lack of it the hemlock of martyrdom.

Several of the critics have given the effect of rubbing their eyes at the phenomenon of being amused by a story essentially tragic. The great scene of Shaw's *Saint Joan* is "full of laughs" while the subject under discussion is the exact judicial and spiritual justification for burning Joan at the stake. The "comedy relief" in Shakespeare's tragedies does not offer the asylum of analogy, for in this play the comedy (let us hope!) is not interlarded; the point of view on the whole tragedy is comic. Must one apologize for this? If man is the only animal who can laugh, need he apologize for his distinction?

S. N. Behrman

May, 1944

JACOBOWSKY AND THE COLONEL *was first produced by The Theatre Guild, in association with Jack H. Skirball, on March 14, 1944, at the Martin Beck Theatre, New York City, with the following cast:*

(In order of appearance)

A YOUNG GIRL	Louise Dowdney
SLEEPING SHOPKEEPER	Harrison Winter
THE TRAGIC GENTLEMAN	Herbert Yost
OLD LADY FROM ARRAS	Jane Marbury
MADAME BOUFFIER	Hilda Vaughn
SOLLY	Harry Davis
SZYCKI	Peter Kass
SZABUNIEWICZ	J. Edward Bromberg
S. L. JACOBOWSKY	Oscar Karlweis
AIR RAID WARDEN	Philip Collier
COLONEL TADEUSZ BOLESLAV STJERBINSKY	Louis Calhern
COSETTE	Kitty Mattern
A CHAUFFEUR	Coby Ruskin
MONSIEUR SEROUILLE	Donald Cameron
MARIANNE	Annabella
BRIGADIER	E. G. Marshall
STREET SINGER	Joseph Kallini
CHILD	Jules Leni
FIRST LIEUTENANT	Frank Overton
GESTAPO OFFICIAL	Harold Vermilyea
WILHELM	Donald Lee
MAX	Bob Merritt
PAPA CLAIRON	Harry Davis
THE DICE PLAYER	Philip Coolidge
SENATOR BRISSON	Donald Cameron
THE COMMISSAIRE	William Sanders
GENDARME	Burton Tripp
SERGEANT DE VILLE	Edward Kreisler

STAGED by Elia Kazan

DESIGNED by Stewart Chaney

MUSIC by Paul Bowles

PRODUCTION UNDER THE SUPERVISION of
Lawrence Langner and Theresa Helburn

The action takes place from June 13th to June 18th, 1940, between Paris and the Atlantic Coast of France.

ACT ONE

ACT ONE

Scene I

SCENE: *The subterranean laundry of the Hotel Mon Repos et de la Rose. It is evening on the 13th of June, 1940. There has been an air-raid alert and the laundry of* MADAME BOUFFIER'S *fourth-class establishment is doing service as an air-raid shelter.*

AT RISE: MADAME BOUFFIER'S *guests have been aroused from their beds by the alert and are trying to find comfort among the functional oddments of the laundry: the pressing and drying machines, the washtubs, etc. Two of the big tin washtubs have been put together and on them is sleeping a stertorous guest. On a long, narrow table along the wall an exhausted soldier and his pretty young wife are doing the same. On the left on a narrow bench by the wall, completely covered with a gray service blanket, is* SZABUNIEWICZ, *the Polish orderly of* COLONEL STJERBINSKY, *fighting off bad dreams.*

The TRAGIC GENTLEMAN, *a faded figure out of Toulouse-Lautrec, all in black with a black cape over his shoulders and wide-brimmed felt hat, is sitting near the washtubs sardonically fending off his despair with an attitude of detachment.*

From the shaded lamps an unearthly blue light bathes the sleepers in violet.

At right a flight of stairs leads up to the sidewalk, and at left another flight leads up into the interior of the hotel. In the distance we hear the buzzing of airplanes.

When the curtain goes up, those guests who are not asleep are listening to a radio announcement by the Prime Minister, Paul Reynaud.

During this speech the OLD LADY FROM ARRAS *comes down the stairs. She is over sixty, pale with fright and sleeplessness, but*

*knits and twitters with a kind of nervous vigor. While the Prime
Minister is speaking, she crosses the stage and sits left on her
special chair which has a cushion on it. She pounds the cushion
into what she conceives to be a comfortable submission and sits
down to her knitting and listens to the radio announcement.*

VOICE OF PRIME MINISTER REYNAUD

. . . The situation is serious but not desperate. On the Somme
our valiant troops are defending every inch of their native soil
with the greatest bravery. However, the superiority of the enemy
in men and material is so great that we must be prepared to
expect . . .

(*The radio groans off.*)

YOUNG GIRL
(*Who is lying beside her sleeping husband*)
Why did the radio go off?

TRAGIC GENTLEMAN
They are forbidden to broadcast during an air raid.

OLD LADY
Who was the gentleman on the radio?

TRAGIC GENTLEMAN
That was our Prime Minister, Monsieur Paul Reynaud, addressing the nation from Bordeaux.

OLD LADY
(*Very anxious*)
But what did he say?

TRAGIC GENTLEMAN
He said the situation was serious but not hopeless, or maybe
he said it was hopeless but not serious.

OLD LADY
Dear God, dear God, Monsieur Paul Reynaud is very far to
the Left. My daughter is a schoolteacher, and she told me. Mon-

sieur Leon Blum wouldn't have anyone work more than forty hours a week. And this is what it brings us to. The last war was better—I understood the last war. This war I don't understand at all. Why, my daughter says, why should we die for Danzig? (*Very militant*) She's right! Why should we?

(MADAME BOUFFIER, *the mistress of the establishment, bustles in. She is wonderfully gotten up: she wears a magenta dress with gold-fringe trimmings; her hair is a marvelously tinted pyramid. She is strident, not unkind, and acts as if her little hotel were Versailles. She carries a lantern, small notebook and pencil. She is followed by* SOLLY, *of whom she is fond and to whom she is tender. He is a white-faced, hunchbacked Jewish boy of eighteen. He also carries a lantern.*)

MADAME BOUFFIER

Solly dear, you haven't drawn those curtains. We don't want to have the same trouble with the Chief Warden we had yesterday.

SOLLY

Yes, Madame Bouffier, at once.

(SOLLY *hangs a lantern on the back wall as* MADAME BOUFFIER *hangs hers on another hook.*)

MADAME BOUFFIER

And I'll check the guests! (*Checking off a list of her guests*) Well, is my little family all here?

OLD LADY
(*Full of self-pity*)

I'm here, Heaven help me.

MADAME BOUFFIER
(*Chiding*)

You should be used to air raids by this time, Madame Arle. In my hotel the morale is high. I am captain of the ship here,

and I want things to be bright and cheerful. That's our way of
defying the Germans. (*In her tour around the room she lifts
blanket from* SZABUNIEWICZ' *head, takes a peek at him and recovers him.*)

OLD LADY
(*Decidedly not cheerful*)

But this is the fourth night I've sat till dawn in this wretched
laundry.

MADAME BOUFFIER
(*With professional pride*)

No hotel in Paris has a more distinguished laundry. You're
lucky to be in it, safe and cozy. (*Continues to check her list.*)

OLD LADY

I just can't believe what's happened. You know I'm from out
of town—from Arras. A few days ago my daughter said, "Mama,
this war is nonsense—it won't last a week." My daughter's a
schoolteacher—and she knows!

MADAME BOUFFIER

Some schoolteachers never learn anything they don't teach.
(*Checking her book*) Madame Gravot—404?

YOUNG GIRL
Here.

MADAME BOUFFIER
And Monsieur Gravot—404?

YOUNG GIRL
(*Caressing her young husband lightly*)
He's asleep.

MADAME BOUFFIER

There! That completes my little family—except for 409 and
204. 409 is that Polish Colonel and 204 is Monsieur Jacobowsky.
Now where is Monsieur Jacobowsky? I've just looked in his

room and he's not there. The Polish Colonel is probably asleep, but where is Monsieur Jacobowsky?

TRAGIC GENTLEMAN

Is that important?

MADAME BOUFFIER

It is indeed important. It's important to our morale in here. I prefer optimism to pessimism. I prefer a sunny day to a cloudy day. Monsieur Jacobowsky has a nature like a sunny day.

TRAGIC GENTLEMAN
(*With mock sadness*)
Monsieur Jacobowsky is your newest paying guest, Madame Bouffier. I am your oldest and yet you appear to prefer Monsieur Jacobowsky to me.

MADAME BOUFFIER

When you describe yourself as a paying guest, Monsieur, you employ poetic license.
(*In the distance the noise of a bomb. A fussy and nervous little man in a meticulously pressed suit comes into the shelter. He wears a pince-nez and carries a brief case and cane. He comes from the street door. As he comes in the sound of ack-ack guns is heard. Then the sound of planes dies out.*)

SZYCKI

I must see Colonel Stjerbinsky.

MADAME BOUFFIER

That's 409. He's probably still in his room.

SZYCKI

During an air raid!

MADAME BOUFFIER

He doesn't take air raids seriously. He sleeps through them.

SZYCKI

It's vital I see him.

MADAME BOUFFIER
(*Indicating* SZABUNIEWICZ)

There's another Pole, his orderly, also asleep. Won't he do?
(SZYCKI *goes to* SZABUNIEWICZ, *kneels down beside him,
prodding him.*)

SZYCKI

Szabuniewicz. Wake up!

SZABUNIEWICZ
(*Captured in a dreadful dream, sprawls, kneeling, to the
floor*)

Take cover . . .

SZYCKI

Szabuniewicz!!

SZABUNIEWICZ

Take cover!

SZYCKI

You've been having a bad dream, my friend. This is Szycki.
(SZABUNIEWICZ *rises. He is rotund, sly, with innocent round
eyes, deeply Machiavellian.*)

SZABUNIEWICZ
(*Rubs his eyes*)

Dream I chased by Messerschmitts.

SZYCKI

Where is the Colonel?

SZABUNIEWICZ
(*Evasive*)

He not here?

SZYCKI

Obviously he is not here.

SZABUNIEWICZ

Den he is somewhere else. (*Folding his blanket.*)

SZYCKI

He is never where you expect to find him. He's never on time. He is irregular—that's what he is—irregular!

SZABUNIEWICZ
(*Sits*)

Colonel irregular—that's what he is.

SZYCKI

And I risked my life to bring him some material.

SZABUNIEWICZ

Give me. I give him.

SZYCKI

Impossible! My orders are to put these documents in the Colonel's hands. . . .

SZABUNIEWICZ

Colonel's hands don't come till Colonel come.

SZYCKI
(*Furious*)

You joking when time is of the essence! The Germans will be here any minute.
(*This statement puts the people in the cellar in a panic.*)

OLD LADY
(*Rises*)

My God, what did he say? The Germans are here?

SOLLY

What did he say?

YOUNG GIRL

He said they are coming! The Germans are coming!

MADAME BOUFFIER

(*Piously*)

May God inspire our generals, Marshal Pétain and General Weygand!

OLD LADY

(*Her voice rises in hysteria*)

The Germans are in Paris. They're in Paris. Dear God! Dear God!

MADAME BOUFFIER

Quiet, Madame Arle. I'll have no panic here. Solly, bring in the gramophone from the salon.

YOUNG GIRL

Wonderful. Let's have a Chevalier record.

TRAGIC GENTLEMAN

Chevalier! He'll give the Germans their idea of Paris. God, how I hate that gigolo!

MADAME BOUFFIER

And, Solly dear, go up to Monsieur Jacobowsky's room. Maybe he has come back.

OLD LADY

If the Germans are in Paris, why do we stay here? Why don't we do something?

(MONSIEUR JACOBOWSKY *comes in through the doorway from the street. He is in his late forties, not tall but somehow not too short—a "small medium." He wears a well-cut lounge suit, which he bought in happier days and which has managed to retain, though it is somewhat shiny, an air of elegance. He has a neat bow tie, a neat voice and everything about him has the crisp edge of tidiness. You feel that in the life he deserted everything in his ménage both business and personal was in good order; that his extra shoes had a good polish; his correspondence was caught up; his desk clear and that when people crossed the threshold of his house to come to dinner they felt a glow of benevolence and the quickened anticipation of a happy evening. His cheerfulness is an emanation from a harried past; he knows that the worst will probably happen, so that your only chance is to improve the immediate present. This he is constantly trying to do in every small relation of life. He likes people and he wants them, if it is at all possible, to like him.)*

JACOBOWSKY

The Germans are not in Paris, Madame, believe me.

SOLLY

Monsieur Jacobowsky!

MADAME BOUFFIER

Oh! Here he is.

JACOBOWSKY

I have just been in the Rue Royale and I assure you there isn't a German in sight. In fact, there isn't even a Parisian in sight. I was the only one in sight.

MADAME BOUFFIER

The Rue Royale! Monsieur Jacobowsky! In the middle of an alert. Suppose something had happened—a falling building or a bomb. . . .

JACOBOWSKY

So there would be one Jacobowsky more or less. The world has endured so much—it could endure that too.

YOUNG GIRL

Monsieur is a very courageous man.

JACOBOWSKY

Not at all, Madame. Only—at one period of my life I was an accountant—and about danger—I am statistical.

TRAGIC GENTLEMAN

No doubt you think that the bomb that will hit *you* has yet
to be cast. It has been cast, believe me. At Krupp or Skoda.

JACOBOWSKY

Oh, I have no doubt. Krupp and Skoda think of me constantly. They cast their little bomb and they think: "This one
we'll send to our nice Jacobowsky." But even Krupp has to yield
to a powerful law—the law of probability. Listen: What is the
population of Paris? Four million lives? Correct? Now what
chance has Krupp, with all his precision work, of hitting one
four-millionth of Paris? Practically non-existent. I tell you I feel
sorry for him. So, moving under the immunity of this adorable
law—I have brought you back some *marrons glacés*—first to our
distinguished hostess. (*Offers* MADAME BOUFFIER *the box.*)

MADAME BOUFFIER

That's my dear Monsieur Jacobowsky—always thinking of
others. (*Takes one.*)

MAN ON THE WASHTUB
(*He is trying to sleep*)

All this shouting—I can't sleep! (*Jumps up—reversing his position, puts his head where his feet were before—and tries to
sleep again.*)

JACOBOWSKY
(*Drops his voice and tiptoes around*)

Please, Madame, allow me . . . (*To the* YOUNG GIRL) Madame . . .

YOUNG GIRL
(*In a whisper*)

Thank you, Monsieur.

OLD LADY
(*Whispering*)

Thank you, Monsieur.

JACOBOWSKY
(*Offering them to* SOLLY)

Solly, friend, you must eat some of these. They'll warm you up.
(*The* WASHTUB MAN *sticks his hand out, the palm open.*
JACOBOWSKY *pops a* marron *into his hand.*)

YOUNG GIRL

Monsieur certainly knows what's delicious.

JACOBOWSKY

People say it's not good to eat between meals, but I would
rather have a snack than a dinner.

MADAME BOUFFIER
(*Looks fondly at* JACOBOWSKY)

Why is it that the best husbands are always unmarried?

JACOBOWSKY
(*Offering* marrons *to the* TRAGIC GENTLEMAN)

Monsieur.

TRAGIC GENTLEMAN

I hate *marrons glacés.* . . .

JACOBOWSKY

They are quite fresh.

TRAGIC GENTLEMAN
(*Determined to be unhappy*)

Especially when they are fresh.

MADAME BOUFFIER
(*With sudden decision*)

Monsieur Jacobowsky, you ought to get married.

JACOBOWSKY
(*Edging away*)

I think maybe not, Madame Bouffier.

MADAME BOUFFIER
(*Advances*)
Why not? Give me one good reason why not?

JACOBOWSKY
(*Retreats*)
You see, Madame Bouffier, I myself am a worshipper of beauty but in my own person I am not quite dazzling. The indifference of the ladies has given me leisure for reading and philosophy. I am a quite well-read man, Madame Bouffier.

MADAME BOUFFIER
You won't know what life is till you get married.

JACOBOWSKY
(*Delicately*)
Perhaps there are other ways of finding out. (*He goes over to the* OLD LADY.)

OLD LADY
Sweets are such a consolation in a situation like this.

JACOBOWSKY
Quite right, Madame—quite right.

OLD LADY
(*Waves her banner*)
My daughter's a schoolteacher!

JACOBOWSKY
(*Sits beside her on stool*)
A noble profession. Aristotle was a schoolteacher.

OLD LADY
In Arras I left everything behind, even my daughter—and fled —fled in France itself! Who could ever imagine a thing like that? While I was doing it, I didn't believe I was doing it and even now, right this minute, I don't believe it.

JACOBOWSKY

Oh, you'll get used to flight. I did. I've spent all my life in a futile effort to become a citizen of some country. You know, I speak seven languages fluently. Wrong, but fluently. In the technique of flight I may say I am a virtuoso. Migration one: Poland to Germany. My poor mother took her five children, her candlesticks, her pillows and fled to Berlin. There I grew up. I was successful in business. I was a citizen, a patriot. I belonged. My mistake! Migration two: Berlin to Vienna! The City of Waltzes. (*Hums one or two bars*) But I soon found out that underneath the waltzes there was a counter-melody. Less charming, more ruthless. First thing you know I was embarked on migration three. Prague. Now Prague is a lovely city. Have you ever seen the lovely baroque architecture in Prague?

TRAGIC GENTLEMAN

I hate baroque!

JACOBOWSKY

I understand that, too. A lot of people very qualified don't like baroque. Still I hated to leave Prague. This time without an overcoat. It was a new experience. Very interesting. Migration four: Paris! City of Light. Here I breathed the air of freedom. I understood exactly how Heine felt when *he* got here. I said to myself: "You are Heine—without the genius." But now I have the feeling that there is ahead of me still another migration. Well, I'm ready. You see, one gets used to it.

OLD LADY

(*Rises, fluffing her chair pillow*)

But after all, Monsieur, between us there isn't any comparison. My family has lived in Arras for five centuries.

JACOBOWSKY

(*Impressed*)

Five centuries! You don't mean it!

OLD LADY
(*Pounding her pillow*)
And now the Boches may push us into the sea. My daughter
is right. She always says, "France needs a Hitler too!"

JACOBOWSKY
(*Rises quietly*)
Don't worry, Madame, your daughter will probably get her
wish—mustache, forelock and all.

MADAME BOUFFIER
I won't have such talk!

OLD LADY
Did I say something wrong?

MADAME BOUFFIER
Your daughter must be insane.

OLD LADY
She's not insane. She's a schoolteacher!

MADAME BOUFFIER
I won't hear such talk.

OLD LADY
Lots of people think so.
(*Police whistle off stage. The* AIR RAID WARDEN *enters ex-
plosively from the street. He is in high dudgeon.*)

WARDEN
Are you out of your mind, Madame Bouffier?

MADAME BOUFFIER
Certainly not! I am in full possession of my faculties.

WARDEN
It's always your hotel I have trouble with. It's your hotel that
is putting all Paris in danger. Fourth floor, street side—second
and third windows from the right. Lit up like a Christmas tree!

MADAME BOUFFIER

Fourth floor, street side? That's 409. That's the Polish Colonel.

WARDEN

I don't care if he's the King of Poland. He's breaking the regulations and it's your responsibility!

MADAME BOUFFIER

I've told him ten times. He doesn't listen. When I tell him, he laughs.

WARDEN

He laughs, does he? He laughs! I'll teach him. I'll teach him to laugh. This is Paris, not Warsaw!

MADAME BOUFFIER

(*Egging him on*)

Why don't you go up and tell him?

WARDEN

I will—I'll more than tell him. I'll teach him a lesson. I'll wipe up the floor with him.

MADAME BOUFFIER

This will be worth watching. Come along, Solly dear. (*She and* SOLLY *follow the* WARDEN *upstairs.*)

THE WASHTUB MAN

Oh, my God, why won't they let me sleep . . . ? (*He abandons the washtubs, wrapped in his blankets, and goes to a corner where he curls up on the floor.*)

SZABUNIEWICZ

Poor Warden. I pity for him.

SZYCKI

It will serve your Colonel right—no matter what the Warden does to him.

SZABUNIEWICZ

I wonder what Colonel do to Warden. Colonel not alone and when he's not alone he wants strictly to be alone.

SZYCKI

So that's what he's doing!

SZABUNIEWICZ

Colonel has always time for romance.

SZYCKI

At a time like this!

SZABUNIEWICZ

Any time good for romance.

SZYCKI

And I have to entrust this mission to a man like that! I'll give him a piece of my mind.

SZABUNIEWICZ

You too—good! Piece of your mind what Colonel needs. Give him big piece.

(*During this scene* JACOBOWSKY *has been sitting quietly reading a worn book which he has taken out of his pocket. The* TRAGIC GENTLEMAN *comes up behind him, curious.*)

TRAGIC GENTLEMAN

May I ask, sir, what you are reading?

JACOBOWSKY

The Ethics of Spinoza.

TRAGIC GENTLEMAN

(*Laughs*)

Ethics! What an anachronism! In the age of the Nazis— Ethics!

JACOBOWSKY

I don't agree. The Nazis are the anachronism—not the ethics! Listen: (*He reads from the book*) "For the wise man, insofar as he is wise, is scarcely ever disturbed in spirit: he is conscious of himself, of God and things as a certain eternal necessity; he never ceases to be and always enjoys satisfaction of mind."

TRAGIC GENTLEMAN

"Satisfaction of mind!" Now! In this moment—when the locusts cover the earth!

JACOBOWSKY

This was not written for special emergencies, sir. It is for all eternity.

TRAGIC GENTLEMAN

And will this help you when the Germans catch you?

JACOBOWSKY

I think so. Did you ever spin a top? The top spins but the center is at rest.

(*At this moment the* WARDEN *comes back, crestfallen.*)

SZABUNIEWICZ

(*Gloating*)

Well, did you wipe up the floor with him?

WARDEN

(*Evidently bewildered by his contact with the* COLONEL)

That Colonel's crazy. No use talking to a crazy man! What kind of a type is that? He's peculiar. I couldn't reach an understanding with him. What's the matter with him? He's dangerous. (*He stalks out through the street door.*)

(MADAME BOUFFIER *comes in, talking to the* COLONEL *who is behind her.*)

MADAME BOUFFIER

And I tell you, Colonel, even if you did fight for France your behavior is unpardonable. (*She comes down the little steps. A moment later the* COLONEL *appears. He is magnificent in his uniform, tall, commanding, saturnine, electric with vitality, euphoric with a sense of his own immemorial authority in the scheme of things. His forehead is bandaged smartly. He follows* MADAME BOUFFIER *down the steps into the laundry.*)

COLONEL
(*Addressing his orderly*)
Szabuniewicz, prepare our departure from Paris.

SZABUNIEWICZ
Yes, Colonel.

COLONEL
(*Whispers a boudoir confidence*)
And, oh, Szabuniewicz, I part from this lovely creature who follows me. Disengage me from her—but—very gracious . . .
(COSETTE, *a pretty French woman of about thirty, comes in. She is a quite sensible person and generally unsentimental—except for the* COLONEL!)

COSETTE
Tadeusz, my darling, if you leave Paris, I go too. . . .

COLONEL
(*Turns to her, rolling smoothly through the routines of gallantry*)
This I tell you. The madrigal of our farewell they have interrupt, but a rose for you will grow always in my heart. Our roads part—perhaps forever—but the memory of your sweet face . . .

MADAME BOUFFIER
(*Cutting in*)
It's all very well for you to be romantic but on account of you the police will padlock my hotel tomorrow.

COLONEL
No. No. They will not. They will lack the time. Tomorrow the police of Paris will be running errands for the Huns!

MADAME BOUFFIER
(*Startled*)

Do you mean, Colonel, that the Germans will meet with no further resistance?

COLONEL

This I know. The regiment I command is force of three thousand men. On the Somme we defend a bridge and for every gun is only eight cartridges. . . .

TRAGIC GENTLEMAN

Where was the French Army?

MADAME BOUFFIER
(*Echoes*)

What happened to our Army?

COLONEL

The German Stukas make black the sky and not one French plane to help us. That I know. . . . On my right and on my left I see the French divisions—fine soldiers—want to fight—have nothing with which to fight—so they are obliged to run—and of my own three thousand Polish boys only is left fifteen. I am their father, and I lose my children—three thousand of them. This I know. This I see. This I feel—here. . . . (*Slaps his heart*) Rather I would be with them, with my children that are gone.

JACOBOWSKY

Then, Colonel, it is your considered opinion that France is lost!

COLONEL

No. She is not lost, Monsieur. She is gift to the German. Charming gift to the German.

(SZABUNIEWICZ *has poured a drink from a pocket flask, which he gives to the* COLONEL. *The* COLONEL *drinks it.*)

TRAGIC GENTLEMAN
(*Valedictory*)

Paris, farewell!
(*At the vision of this disaster the* OLD LADY *sways.*)

OLD LADY
(*About to faint*)

I don't feel very well. I don't feel . . .

JACOBOWSKY
(*Goes to her, grips her arm to sustain her*)

Courage, Madame. My poor mother, wise woman that she was, always used to say that no matter what happens in life there are always two possibilities. It is true. For example, right now it is a dark moment and yet even now there are two possibilities. The Germans—either they'll come to Paris or they'll jump to England. If they don't come to Paris, that's good. But if they should come to Paris, again there are two possibilities. Either we succeed in escaping, or we don't succeed. If we succeed, that's good, but if we don't there are always two possibilities. The Germans, either they'll put us in a good concentration camp or in a bad concentration camp. If in a good concentration camp that's good, but if they put us in a bad concentration camp, there are still two . . .

TRAGIC GENTLEMAN
(*Catching him up*)

Two fine possibilities. Jump in the river or be shot by the Boches. Paris, farewell!
(*In spite of* JACOBOWSKY'S *optimism, the* OLD LADY FROM ARRAS *promptly faints. Some of the guests form a closely packed knot around her, trying to revive her.* COSETTE, *in her personal coil, pleads with the* COLONEL.)

COSETTE

And for us, Tadeusz, is there no longer any possibility for us?

COLONEL

My lovely friend, this is what I am about to tell you when they interrupt—since last I saw you I have fallen in love . . .

COSETTE

I knew it—the moment I saw you—I knew there was something. I knew it.

COLONEL

And for you my feeling is so tender, so precious, that I cannot give you less than myself for you deserve all.

COSETTE
(*Fatalistic*)

I knew it. . . .
(SZABUNIEWICZ *sidles up to the* COLONEL.)

SZABUNIEWICZ

Please, Colonel.

COLONEL
(*Shouts*)

What, Szabuniewicz?

SZABUNIEWICZ
(*Indicates* SZYCKI; *he enjoys the prospect of battle*)
This gentleman here waiting for you. He angry. He says you are irregular.

COLONEL
(*Lofty*)

What interest that to me?

SZABUNIEWICZ

Has very strong mind. Wants to give you piece.

COLONEL

I hope he has for me something less mediocre.

SZYCKI

I have the documents for which you wait.

COLONEL
(*Holds out imperious hand*)
Then give.

SZYCKI
(*Hands him yellow oblong envelope*)
Here it is.

COLONEL
Everything here?

SZYCKI
Everything in code. Addresses of our men in Warsaw, Lodz and Cracow. Every plan and communication is there. You must get it to our government in London.

COLONEL
I bring it to London.

SZYCKI
In the Café of Papa Clairon in St. Jean de Luz you meet the man with the gray gloves.

COLONEL
(*Nods*)
Gray gloves.

SZYCKI
He will give you passage on corvette with other of our people to London.

COLONEL
I meet him when?

SZYCKI
On the 18th in the afternoon.

COLONEL
(*Refuses to clutter his mind with tedious detail*)
Szabuniewicz, how many days away is the 18th?

SZABUNIEWICZ
(*Promptly*)

Six days.

COLONEL

I deliver the papers.

SZYCKI

I must impress upon you, sir, time is of the essence.

COLONEL

I must impress upon you, my desk bureaucrat, that you speak to one of Pilsudski's Colonels. I deliver these papers my own method, my own way, my own time.

SZYCKI

The corvette won't wait for you. If you're not there on the afternoon of the 18th it sails without you.

COLONEL

Then let him sail. If necessary, I swim to London.

SZYCKI

I have obeyed my orders. The papers are in your hands. (*He starts to go.*)

COLONEL
(*Shouts after him*)

You go back to your bureau, give orders to your office boy, not to Tadeusz Boleslav Stjerbinsky. Szabuniewicz, we leave Paris now.

SZABUNIEWICZ

How?

COLONEL

I take plane.

SZABUNIEWICZ

The last plane leaved yesterday night.

COLONEL

Then I go by car.

SZABUNIEWICZ

Vice-consul go off yesterday night. He take all four cars.

COLONEL

Why that pig need four cars?

SZABUNIEWICZ

I don't know.

COLONEL

If no car, get me horse.

SZABUNIEWICZ

Horse!

COLONEL

Why not? In one day good horse cover so many kilometers as one medium tank. Pack my trunk, everything you see. (*As* SZA-BUNIEWICZ *turns to obey*) Wait! Szabuniewicz, child—my rosary! Don't forget my rosary!

(SZABUNIEWICZ *goes upstairs.*)

MADAME BOUFFIER
(*Calls after him*)

And don't forget not to put the light on!

COLONEL

Not to worry, Madame. My man find everything in the dark.
(*The* COLONEL *finds himself unexpectedly confronted by* JACOBOWSKY. *He stares at him.*)

JACOBOWSKY

Colonel, my name is Jacobowsky—S. L. Jacobowsky—in a certain sense a countryman. I, too, was born in Poland.

COLONEL
(*Turns away after a sharp glance*)

About that—there is nothing I can do.

JACOBOWSKY

(*As if he had been encouraged*)

Inadvertently I heard you discuss with my other countryman means of locomotion. Do I understand, Colonel, that it is important for you to leave Paris?

COLONEL

(*Spinning around*)

Monsieur, what your name was?

JACOBOWSKY

Jacobowsky, by your leave.

COLONEL

You eavesdrop on our conversation.

JACOBOWSKY

Eavesdrop? Why do I have to eavesdrop when I hear without eavesdropping? Now my suggestion is that possibly—we can get a car in which to leave Paris.

COLONEL

We?

JACOBOWSKY

The good Madame Bouffier here, she has spoken to me of a car for sale . . .

COLONEL

This no doubt very convenient for you but how does it concern me?

JACOBOWSKY

If the car were available we might take it together.

COLONEL

You persist in the use of this intimate pronoun "we." When I travel, I travel alone. When I travel with company it is company that I choose.

JACOBOWSKY

An admirable way to travel. And from my side, I would choose you gladly—because you are a strong man—you are a chivalrous man. Now I have to provide you with a reason why you should choose me. If you will forgive me for saying so, I am a resourceful man. Strength plus resourcefulness! Isn't it a good combination for an emergency like this? Tell me frankly, sir, your opinion.

COLONEL

I do not understand your mentality. (*He turns to* COSETTE, *takes her in his arms*) When the alarm stop, my man will take you home.

COSETTE

But I don't want to go home. I want to stay with you. I want to stay with you forever.

COLONEL

My sweet child—this is not possible.

COSETTE
(*Bursts out*)

Who is she—that you love?

COLONEL

And what will it avail you to know? How can I convey to you the tenderness I feel for you, the fragrance your image invokes in me . . . (*With an impulsive gesture he removes a decoration from his tunic, holds it out to her*) Do you know what this is, my child? It is the Grand Cross of the Order of St. George. It is yours!

COSETTE

I don't want your medal. I want you.

COLONEL

This is the best of me. When I received it, I wept. It is yours.
(SZABUNIEWICZ *returns.*)

SZABUNIEWICZ

Everything prepared to go, Colonel.

COLONEL

Szabuniewicz, you take my sweet friend here home safe . . .
(SZABUNIEWICZ *comes forward eagerly, a gleam in his eye.*)

SZABUNIEWICZ

Yes, Colonel.

COSETTE

I'd rather go alone, thank you. (*Her eyes meet the* COLONEL's.
She sees it is hopeless) I won't forget you—not in a thousand
years. . . . (*She starts upstairs*) Good-bye.

COLONEL

Farewell, Cosette. (*As she exits—in an ecstasy of romantic
dramatization*) In the cathedral of my soul a candle burns for
you, a flame that will never go out.

(COSETTE *is gone. The* COLONEL *looks at* SZABUNIEWICZ,
clucking appreciation of his own gift for romantic rhetoric.
SZABUNIEWICZ *clucks back admiringly.* JACOBOWSKY, *now
that the coast is clear, approaches the* COLONEL *again.*)

JACOBOWSKY

Forgive me, sir, but may we resume our conversation?

COLONEL

Oh! You are Monsieur Wolfsohn—no?

JACOBOWSKY

Yes, Jacobowsky—if you don't mind. My mother always used
to say, no matter how hopeless things look, there are always two
possibilities.

COLONEL
(*Flatly*)

I disagree with your mother.

JACOBOWSKY

I can prove it mathematically.

COLONEL

Why you speak to me mathematically? Hear me, Monsieur
Wolfsohn, for a true man is one possibility.

JACOBOWSKY

That's not enough. With one possibility I can't maneuver.

COLONEL

I repeat, Monsieur Wolfsohn, for a man of honor one possibility.

JACOBOWSKY

If that were true, I would be dead, I don't know how many
times. Now—let us assume for the sake of argument—that we
acquire this car . . .

COLONEL

Again you assume that we are engaged in a joint enterprise,
and this is an exaggeration. I do not know you, Monsieur . . .

JACOBOWSKY

(*His voice rises a little desperately*)

I must tell you, sir, that this may be the last chance to get a
car in Paris. . . .

COLONEL

Then I go on horseback.

JACOBOWSKY

You will never be in St. Jean de Luz on the 18th if you travel
on horseback.

COLONEL

Psiav Krev—you eavesdrop this too! (*In a kind of despair*)
Szabuniewicz, disengage me from this fellow.

(SZABUNIEWICZ *rushes to* JACOBOWSKY *and urges him away
from the* COLONEL. *At this moment the sirens howl. The
alert is over.* SOLLY *and the* YOUNG GIRL *support the* OLD

LADY FROM ARRAS, *helping her out. This outgoing torrent carries along with it* JACOBOWSKY, *who, as he is swept away, cries out exhortations to the* COLONEL. *Finally they all disappear. The* COLONEL *and* SZABUNIEWICZ *are left alone.*)

COLONEL
(*To* SZABUNIEWICZ)

Szabuniewicz, my sword! The affrontery of this fellow. Every rebuff he takes for an invitation.

SZABUNIEWICZ
(*Buckling on the* COLONEL's *sword—the opportunist*)

Still, if he should get a comfortable car . . .

COLONEL

Out of the question. You know I travel alone.

SZABUNIEWICZ
(*Temporizing—it would solve his problem if* JACOBOWSKY *got a car and the* COLONEL *would take it*)

Yes, I know—I know.

COLONEL

Well—what are you waiting for?

SZABUNIEWICZ

I am formulating my plans.

COLONEL

Marianne awaits me at St. Cyrille.

SZABUNIEWICZ
(*Aghast*)

St. Cyrille!

COLONEL

St. Cyrille.

SZABUNIEWICZ

But that is north!

COLONEL

Of course it's north. Did you think that I thought it was east, or west or south?

SZABUNIEWICZ

But that is where the Germans are!

COLONEL

Since when I fear the Germans? Marianne awaits me. No obstacle stops me—no German—no Germans. (*Exalted by his own romantic Quixoticism he starts for the stairs, shouting aloud his affirmation*) Marianne—I come—to you! (*He is gone.*)

SZABUNIEWICZ

(*In a panic runs after him, importuning wildly*)

But, Colonel! St. Cyrille! Colonel, I beg you . . . St. Cyrille! Colonel!

Curtain

ACT ONE

Scene II

Scene: *The little square outside the Hotel Mon Repos et de la Rose. It is very early in the morning; a vista of old Paris buildings, in the distance a church, all gleaming in the pearly iridescence of dawn. A crested and polished Renault limousine stands before the entrance to* MADAME BOUFFIER'S *hotel.*

When the curtain goes up a CHAUFFEUR *in a violet uniform is expatiating to* JACOBOWSKY *on the miracles of this car. The chauffeur's uniform is impeccable. His face, however, is a study in stupidity and cunning.*

CHAUFFEUR
(With corrupt candor)
I would ask Monsieur to consider nothing but the plain facts. Facts are facts, as they say. Now where are the Germans? At Meaux! Which way are they marching? This way! Tomorrow they'll be marching up the Champs Elysées. What an optimist I am! This *evening!*

JACOBOWSKY
(His patience nearly gone)
Come to the point, please. . . .

CHAUFFEUR
The Germans will enter Paris from west-*north*west. Whereas, here before you stands one of the most faithful autos in France, ready to drive you west-*south*west.

JACOBOWSKY
Come to the point, if you please. . . .

CHAUFFEUR

The point is you should thank your lucky stars that I came along like this. There's not another car left in Paris! Even the few taxis that are left are hiding away since yesterday. Try to get a cab, Monsieur. (JACOBOWSKY *starts to go. The* CHAUFFEUR *pulls him back*) Just try and see what happens. And suppose you found another car—where would you get the gasoline? Where would that blood of life come from to fill the hungry tank? (*Abruptly*) Are you sick? Monsieur, you know, you look sick.

JACOBOWSKY

Who looks well so early in the morning? Well, it's possible I'm nervous today.

CHAUFFEUR

Keep up your morale! Swat your wife twice a day—that always helps morale.

JACOBOWSKY

About this car . . .

CHAUFFEUR

This car comes from a very distinguished stable. Guess which one.

JACOBOWSKY

No guessing games, please. No guessing games.

CHAUFFEUR

(*Playing his trump card*)

Rothschild!

JACOBOWSKY

The Baron Rothschild? (*He whistles.*)

CHAUFFEUR

Don't you recognize this crest? Monsieur, in this car you will travel like a king.

JACOBOWSKY

I don't want to be so conspicuous.

CHAUFFEUR

Just before he left, the Baron shook hands with me. He said, "Philbert, it is true that I am particularly attached to this car. . . ."

JACOBOWSKY

Come to the point. What do you want? I have been listening to you talk for twenty minutes. Your wife and children are as familiar to me as my own face. I know what you like to eat and drink, what paper you read! *But what do you want for this car?*

CHAUFFEUR

(*Not to be rushed*)

The rubber satisfies you, I take it?

JACOBOWSKY

It's rubber.

CHAUFFEUR

The tank is filled to the brim with gasoline, I mentioned that?

JACOBOWSKY

You did.

CHAUFFEUR

And the Mobiloil?

JACOBOWSKY

You mentioned that too.

CHAUFFEUR

And that there are three more cans in the back, free of charge?

JACOBOWSKY

You've told me three times.

CHAUFFEUR

And you realize by now, Monsieur, you're the luckiest man in Paris?

JACOBOWSKY

Stop envying me and tell me the price.

CHAUFFEUR

And on my side, I feel almost certain the Baron would be happy to have you as his successor. All in all, adding all these facts together—there is really nothing more to say.

JACOBOWSKY

Just the same I'm sure you'll say it. Well?

CHAUFFEUR

Monsieur, this superb vehicle will cost you a mere fleabite— forty thousand francs.

JACOBOWSKY
(*Sways*)

Don't lift me till I fall . . .

CHAUFFEUR

Morale, Monsieur. Keep it up!
(*But* JACOBOWSKY *washes his hands of the negotiations. He starts away.*)

JACOBOWSKY

Thank you very much for your trouble. Good-bye.

CHAUFFEUR
(*Follows him in a panic*)

Monsieur, I await your counter proposals. . . . Did I say forty? I really meant thirty.

JACOBOWSKY
(*Temporizes*)

I want to buy this car. You want to sell it. Fact?

CHAUFFEUR

Fact.

JACOBOWSKY

You told me the Germans will be here any minute. They will requisition this car. Fact? Fact! You have to sell it or dump it in the river. Fact? Fact! Does it have a spare tire? No! And look at the tires on the wheels. . . . (*Kicking one*) That has seen a good thirty thousand miles!

CHAUFFEUR

Not fifteen, Monsieur!

JACOBOWSKY
(*Riding over him*)
And under the hood— (*Lifts up hood of car*) My God, what is going on in there! Black and greasy! A regular Dante's Inferno in there! (*He closes the hood.*)

CHAUFFEUR
(*Hurt*)
Excuse me, that motor works like my own heart!

JACOBOWSKY

And how do I know you haven't got a heart condition? All in all, this venerable monument isn't worth ten thousand francs!

CHAUFFEUR
(*Aghast*)
Monsieur!

JACOBOWSKY

Attention, Monsieur! Are you *legally* authorized to sell this car? I smell here a most irregular transaction—final price fifteen thousand! (*He counts out money.*)

CHAUFFEUR

Monsieur. For the sake of my children . . .

JACOBOWSKY
(*Adds an extra banknote*)
For the sake of your children, sixteen thousand.

CHAUFFEUR

You are over-reaching an old soldier of Verdun . . .

JACOBOWSKY
(*Adds additional banknote*)

For the sake of Verdun, seventeen thousand. (*Gives* CHAUF-
FEUR *money.*)

CHAUFFEUR
(*Accepting the bills*)

Now you see how weak we Frenchmen are. The Nazis are
right—that's our damned decadence for you! The ownership
license . . . (*Gives him license*) As soon as you sign your name
the Baron's limousine is yours. (*Handing him key*) Here is the
ignition key. . . .

JACOBOWSKY
(*Taking it*)

Ignition key? What do you do with the ignition key?

CHAUFFEUR
(*Surprised*)

Monsieur, in the lock, you . . . (JACOBOWSKY *tries to fit the
ignition key in the keyhole of the door of the car*) You don't
know what you do with the ignition key?

JACOBOWSKY

It now occurs to me that I don't know how to drive. At home
I always had a driver.

CHAUFFEUR
(*Edging away*)

You'll find someone.

JACOBOWSKY

What are *you* doing today? I mean, would your wife permit
you to leave Paris for a few days?

CHAUFFEUR

Out of the question, Monsieur. I have to sell two more cars
before the Germans arrive.

JACOBOWSKY

Rothschild's too?

CHAUFFEUR

(*Pointing to the* TRAGIC GENTLEMAN, *who has just come out of the hotel*)

Maybe he'll drive your car.

(*Under his broad, capelike coat the* TRAGIC GENTLEMAN *carries a modest piece of luggage. He takes a few deep breaths as if to fill his lungs with Paris air for the last time.*)

JACOBOWSKY

Good morning, sir. Can you drive a car?

TRAGIC GENTLEMAN

How does that concern you?

JACOBOWSKY

It seems to me you fill your lungs with the air of Paris as if for the last time.

TRAGIC GENTLEMAN
(*Sadly*)

Yes, I am leaving Paris.

JACOBOWSKY

Any conveyance?

TRAGIC GENTLEMAN

My legs.

JACOBOWSKY

Would you care to come with me? I have just bought a car. Now if you can drive, you could reach your destination much faster.

(MADAME BOUFFIER *comes in, stands on stoop, watching the scene.*)

TRAGIC GENTLEMAN

Destination is a sixth sense, but only great men, artists and statesmen have it. I have no destination.

JACOBOWSKY

Wouldn't you rather ride to it?

TRAGIC GENTLEMAN

No. I shall continue on foot like everyone else. There, you hear them . . .

> (*In the distance the confused tramping of footsteps is now heard.*)

JACOBOWSKY
(*Pale*)

The Germans?

TRAGIC GENTLEMAN

No, the Parisians.

CHAUFFEUR

> (*Lounging about out of curiosity; he has no cars to sell. He is simply lazy*)

Yes, that's the Parisians all right.

TRAGIC GENTLEMAN

Walking, walking, walking. They are marching to the stations but the stations are dead—no trains move out—so they turn about and walk through the long rows of suburbs—a thousand, ten thousand, one hundred thousand—all with bag and baggage. What is kept of life animates the legs and they walk and walk. Where we shall be when the Boches arrive only God and St. Denis know! Listen! (*The sound of the rolling of shutters*) The last metal shutters rolling down to blind the shop windows. Lafayette and Potin and the smart little jewel boxes in the Rue de la Paix. When the Boches march in, Paris will be a dirty coffin, a coffin without a corpse. But I was born in Paris and to Paris I belong and I'm moving with the people of Paris out of Paris and I want to walk not drive—walk with all the others—

with the moving boulevards, day after day—hour after hour. When your legs ache, the heart doesn't ache so much. (*He goes out.* JACOBOWSKY *gazes after him, spellbound. In his trance he muses aloud.*)

JACOBOWSKY

He knows his destination—to be at one with the other Parisians; and my destination—like the Greeks of Xenophon—Thalata! (MADAME BOUFFIER *walks over to him. She is concerned and mystified.* JACOBOWSKY *explains to her*) Thalata! That's what the ancient Greeks called the sea. Because on the sea there are ships and these ships sail to England and to America. (*He looks around in desperation and appeals to the* CHAUFFEUR *again*) Won't you drive me to the sea?

CHAUFFEUR
(*Gaily*)
Impossible, Monsieur, my mother is dying.
(*In the background an* OLD MAN *and a* LITTLE BOY *walk by. The* OLD MAN *carries his belongings in a few bags and hums a street song. Other stragglers pass by.*)

MADAME BOUFFIER
(*As she looks at them*)
At last it's happening. Everyone is deserting me. Everyone is leaving Paris—and now you, too, my dear Monsieur Jacobowsky. My house is empty—only the mice and the water bugs and those two Poles are left. I have no courage any more. Just imagine, Monsieur Jacobowsky, at thirty-five I am a broken, old woman. (*Skeptical guffaw from the* CHAUFFEUR. MADAME BOUFFIER *is furious*) What are you laughing at, you scamp? Thirty-five in May. Do you want to see my birth certificate?

JACOBOWSKY
(*Consoling her*)
You have a young heart, Madame Bouffier.

MADAME BOUFFIER

Did you buy the car from this robber?
(MADAME BOUFFIER *and* CHAUFFEUR *snarl at each other.*)

JACOBOWSKY
(*Leading her out of controversy*)
Thank you for bringing him to me. Here is a warehouse list
—old furniture I bought before the war—I had a dream of fur-
nishing my own apartment. Take it. There are some nice things.
Decorate your house with them.

MADAME BOUFFIER
(*Accepting warehouse list*)
I'll keep it for you. One day you'll find a beautiful woman
who will love you and I'll give her your furniture.

JACOBOWSKY
(*Dismissing the possibility*)
A beautiful woman doesn't need my furniture. Where are my
things?

MADAME BOUFFIER
(*Calling*)
Solly dear, Monsieur Jacobowsky's things!

JACOBOWSKY
It seems foolish, but I'm very much attached to those two
Teheran rugs. They're museum pieces. At least I'll take with
me the illusion of a charming home.
(SOLLY *enters staggering under the rugs.*)

MADAME BOUFFIER
(*Indicating* CHAUFFEUR)
Is he driving you south to the sea?

CHAUFFEUR
What would I do at the sea! I'm a Parisian!

JACOBOWSKY
(*To* SOLLY)

Solly dear, I am worried about you. What will become of you if the Germans come?

SOLLY
(*Depositing his load in the car*)

I'd rather not think about it. . . .

MADAME BOUFFIER
(*With emotion*)

I make myself responsible for him—if I have to lock him in the cellar and stand guard.

(*The* COLONEL'S *voice is heard off stage berating* SZABUNIE-WICZ.)

COLONEL

Szabuniewicz, I have told you over and over again, you must provide transportation. Where is it?

(SZABUNIEWICZ *and* COLONEL STJERBINSKY *now come out of the hotel.* SZABUNIEWICZ *is carrying a bulging officer's knapsack and saddle bags. Under one arm the* COLONEL *has a violin case.*)

SZABUNIEWICZ

This question I fail to solve, Colonel.

COLONEL

Did you think we would remain in Paris forever? You should have thought about it, Szabuniewicz.

SZABUNIEWICZ

I think—but nothing comes. (*Drops baggage on the floor.*)

COLONEL

I told you a car, a horse, a carriage—anything. Where are they?

SZABUNIEWICZ

Give me time, Colonel. I will solve it.

COLONEL

Time! There is no time! Time is of the . . . (*Automatically he finds himself repeating the hated phrase. He stops and at the same moment he takes in the Rothschild limousine.*)

(JACOBOWSKY *points dramatically to the car.*)

JACOBOWSKY
(*Quietly*)

There she stands, Colonel.

COLONEL

What is to me—that she stands? Let her stand. (*To* SZABUNIE-WICZ) You say no car is left in Paris—here is car.

SZABUNIEWICZ
(*Who is dying for the deal to go through—this will solve all his problems*)

Maybe I can negotiate . . .

JACOBOWSKY

Why negotiate? You are welcome to it. (*To* COLONEL) You remember, perhaps, our conversation?

COLONEL

I remember no conversation.

JACOBOWSKY

Are you by any chance an automobilist?

COLONEL
(*Elegantly*)

I am cavalryist. . . .

JACOBOWSKY
(*Pleasantly*)

But modern cavalry is generally motorized.

COLONEL
(*With simple pride*)

In Poland—no!

JACOBOWSKY
(*Noticing violin case*)

You are a violinist?

COLONEL

I fiddle.

JACOBOWSKY

You are fond of chamber music?

COLONEL
(*Isolated*)

I fiddle solo.

JACOBOWSKY

Can you drive a car—solo?

COLONEL

If road is correct and straight I can drive. Curves I don't care to see.

JACOBOWSKY

Perhaps on the curves, we can compromise.

COLONEL
(*With sudden recognition*)

I remember you now—you are Monsieur Leibowicz.

JACOBOWSKY
(*Pleased with his accuracy*)

Yes, Jacobowsky.

COLONEL

You are Pole?

JACOBOWSKY

I was born in Poland. It is the first of my native lands.

COLONEL
(*Interested*)

Where in Poland were you born?

JACOBOWSKY

In the village of Studno near Kasimisz.

COLONEL
(*The recognition becomes almost intimate*)
So—Studno near Stanislau.

SZABUNIEWICZ
(*Helping along*)
Good locality!

COLONEL
My father had great estates there. Owned many villages. Your papa, a dealer in liquid spirits, no doubt?

JACOBOWSKY
Not spirits—spirit!—and not liquid. He taught the children Biblical history.

COLONEL
Good profession.

SZABUNIEWICZ
(*All for the intellect*)
Very educational.

COLONEL
(*Mumbles an inventory to reassure himself*)
From the village of Studno near Kasimisz—father schoolteacher—understands music . . .

JACOBOWSKY
(*Feeling the moment has come for the* coup de grace)
Perhaps it might be interesting, sir, for us to travel together.

COLONEL
Interesting? How interesting?

JACOBOWSKY
Psychologically. You are—if I may make so bold—cast suddenly in a new role. Instead of being in the enviable position of persecuting other people, you are persecuted yourself. Now I'm used to that and I'll help you get used to it too.

COLONEL
(*A bit put off*)
I need no help from you, Monsieur.

JACOBOWSKY
Probably not—but if you should want it, there I'll be.

COLONEL
If I consent drive your car, it is because it help me bring out from danger vital documents of our Polish motherland's fight for freedom.

JACOBOWSKY
(*Humoring him*)
Do not deny me the privilege of assisting in a patriotic act.

COLONEL
(*Struck by this*)
Ah! You would be patriot?

JACOBOWSKY
(*Firm*)
My deepest ambition.

COLONEL
(*With a spasm of tolerance*)
Cannot deny man right to be patriot.

SZABUNIEWICZ
(*Godly*)
That would be sin.

COLONEL
(*He has made the great decision. He turns to* JACOBOWSKY)
Monsieur, I will drive your car!

JACOBOWSKY
(*Overcome*)
Colonel! If it weren't for your rank, I'd embrace you.
(*The* COLONEL *stops any overtures with an upraised hand.*

Then he turns to inspect the car, sees JACOBOWSKY's *rugs in the back seat.*)

COLONEL

First, come out from this car these rugs. (*He puts his violin in the back seat of the car.*)

JACOBOWSKY

Excuse me, Colonel, these rugs mean very much to me.

COLONEL

Excuse me, please. I am one of Pilsudski's Colonels! I not used to voyage in furniture truck. No, the backside must remain empty.

JACOBOWSKY

And why must the backside remain empty?

COLONEL

I am not used to give reasons.

SZABUNIEWICZ
(*Explaining*)

We travel light.

MADAME BOUFFIER
(*Intervenes*)

But it's his car . . .

COLONEL

Monsieur . . . (*To* SZABUNIEWICZ) What's his name?

MADAME BOUFFIER
(*Shouting it*)

Jacobowsky!

COLONEL

Monsieur Jacobowsky. In this car you carry out not only your small self but you serve high purpose—maybe for first time in your life—no?

SZABUNIEWICZ

You help Poland.

JACOBOWSKY

Can't I help Poland and take my rugs too?

SZABUNIEWICZ
(*Whispers*)

Be careful—you'll irritate him.

COLONEL
(*He is irritated*)

You see, Szabuniewicz, what means to take favor from certain people. (*He walks away, whispering imprecations to himself.*)

SZABUNIEWICZ

You did irritate him!

JACOBOWSKY
(*After a mournful pause*)

Solly dear, take the rugs out of the car. (*As* SOLLY *obeys*) Madame Bouffier, please keep these rugs as a further acknowledgment of my debt to you.

(SZABUNIEWICZ *keeps piling the* COLONEL's *paraphernalia into the car.*)

MADAME BOUFFIER
(*Outraged—to* JACOBOWSKY)

My dear, why do you stand for it?

JACOBOWSKY

There are two things a man shouldn't be angry at—what he can help and what he can't help.

(MADAME BOUFFIER *catches sight of the* COLONEL *engaged in a violent controversy with himself.*)

MADAME BOUFFIER

Look! He's talking to himself. The moment he stamped into my house I knew he was out of his mind.

JACOBOWSKY

You're wrong, Madame Bouffier. A man who talks to himself is usually lonely. I have the most charming conversations with myself.

SZABUNIEWICZ

(*Everything having been cleared, he opens the front door of the car*)

Take place, gentlemen—Boches is on the march.

(COLONEL *gets in the front seat, sits there stiffly.* JACOBOWSKY *comes forward with an automobile map.*)

JACOBOWSKY

Our route is main boulevard, Place de la Bastille, Ivry, and down the Route Nationale west-southwest.

COLONEL

You are wrong, Yalofsky—our way go down the Champs Elysées, Neuilly, Saint-Cloud and Route Nationale west-*north*west.

JACOBOWSKY

(*To* SZABUNIEWICZ, *easily*)

I am sure the Colonel means west-*south*west.

SZABUNIEWICZ

(*With a malicious grin*)

No. Colonel means west-*north*west.

JACOBOWSKY

(*Stunned as he sees the* COLONEL's *set face*)

Northwest! (*Turns to* SZABUNIEWICZ) Is there something wrong with my hearing?

SZABUNIEWICZ

Be careful—you'll irritate him.

JACOBOWSKY

Did he say *north*west?

SZABUNIEWICZ

That's what he said. And that's where we go.

JACOBOWSKY

But *north*west—there are the German divisions— (*To* MADAME BOUFFIER) right into the arms of . . .

SZABUNIEWICZ
(*Warning him*)

Leave it to him.
(*A silence.* JACOBOWSKY *struggles with this appalling fact. He advances toward the car and addresses the statue of the* COLONEL.)

JACOBOWSKY
(*Tentatively*)

Colonel dear—I don't ask for a shoe larger than my foot but, after all, it is my car, isn't it? (*Suddenly uncertain, he turns to the* CHAUFFEUR) Did I buy this car from you or didn't I?

CHAUFFEUR

You bought it all right.

SZABUNIEWICZ
(*Increased warning*)

Be careful!

JACOBOWSKY

But it is *my* car.

MADAME BOUFFIER
(*Shouts*)

But it's his car.

JACOBOWSKY
(*Points to* CHAUFFEUR)

There is the evidence.

COLONEL
(*Rises in mighty anger*)

My car! What means that? On a stormy sea you say, "This lifeboat is my lifeboat?" The devil take you—to hell you go. (*He*

stamps out of the car and flings a command to SZABUNIEWICZ)
Szabuniewicz! Horses! (*He goes off.*)
    (*The lifeline is cut! The others stand frozen in silence.*
SZABUNIEWICZ *is the first to emerge.*)

SZABUNIEWICZ

I told you to be careful—when he says *north*west, he means
*north*west.

JACOBOWSKY

Evidently.

SZABUNIEWICZ

We go first to pick up lady.

JACOBOWSKY

Lady? What kind of lady?

SZABUNIEWICZ
(*Looking foxy*)

Lady-love.

MADAME BOUFFIER
(*To* JACOBOWSKY)

My dear, can't you find another driver?
    (*The* COLONEL *comes back. Locked in his indignation he
stands apart, his arms crossed over his chest. He waits for
the world to conciliate him.* JACOBOWSKY *looks at him.*)

JACOBOWSKY
(*To* MADAME BOUFFIER)

Just a minute . . . (*Clears his throat, whispers to* SZABUNIE-
WICZ) Any lady who would interest the Colonel to such an
extent where he risks his life and documents—well—she must be
a very rare person.

SZABUNIEWICZ

Of course!
    (*A silence.* JACOBOWSKY *approaches the* COLONEL.)

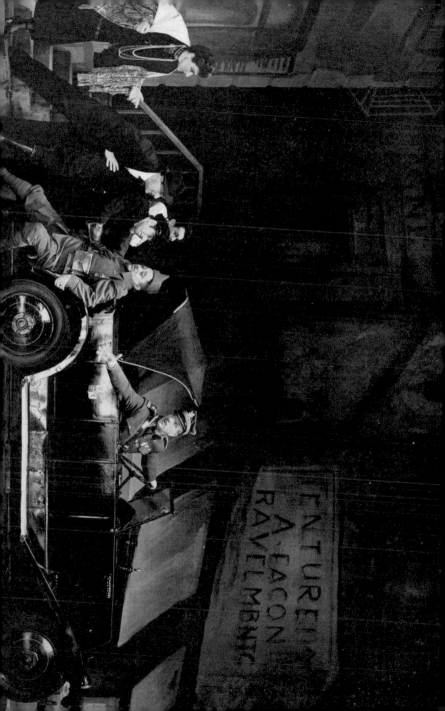

JACOBOWSKY

Any use to talk to you about this?

COLONEL

No use!

SZABUNIEWICZ
(*Echoes*)

No use!

COLONEL
(*The auctioneer's last announcement*)

Time is fleeting.

JACOBOWSKY
(*Helplessly, to* MADAME BOUFFIER)

No use. (*He turns to* COLONEL *and concedes all*) Colonel.
You're right! You are a strategist. You have a plan. If you say
west-*north*west you have an idea in it—and I agree. Which direction you like, I agree. I agree. I agree.

(*The* COLONEL *clamps him on the shoulder as if bestowing
an accolade for his good sense but the accolade quickly
becomes a violent push.* JACOBOWSKY *finds himself in the*
CHAUFFEUR'S *lap. Meantime the* COLONEL *has resumed his
place in the car.* JACOBOWSKY *recovers his balance, runs to*
MADAME BOUFFIER *and to* SOLLY, *embracing them.*)

JACOBOWSKY

Good-bye, dear Madame Bouffier. Good-bye, Solly friend.
Good-bye in all seven languages.

MADAME BOUFFIER

Good luck. Good luck, dear friend.

(JACOBOWSKY *runs toward the car. The* COLONEL *steps sav-
agely on the accelerator, but the car does not react. He
begins to swear.*)

COLONEL

What dirty thing is this? I give spurs to the villain but she
don't move.

JACOBOWSKY
(*Shouts to the* CHAUFFEUR)
The motor is a fake!

CHAUFFEUR
Would I be standing here if the motor was a fake? The battery needs recharging, that's all. There is a garage twenty meters away. Everybody out and push . . .

COLONEL
(*Scowling*)
Now, you see, Jacobowsky, what complications come with you?

SZABUNIEWICZ
(*Bitter*)
And is only now the beginning.

CHAUFFEUR
(*His sleeves pushed up*)
Push, gentlemen, push.
(*The* CHAUFFEUR, JACOBOWSKY, SZABUNIEWICZ *and* SOLLY *all start pushing the car from the rear fender. The* COLONEL *sits at the wheel, his grandeur undimmed when suddenly he feels the need to invoke a higher power. He rises to his great height, addressing, without turning to look at them, the little strugglers at the rear of the car.*)

COLONEL
Stop! Nobody knows what lies before us. Therefore I think is wise to call upon the Heaven before we start on the undertaking. (SZABUNIEWICZ *jumps into an attitude of devotion, takes off his hat and puts his hand over his eyes. The* CHAUFFEUR *also attempts to look other-worldly.* JACOBOWSKY *doesn't know quite what to do. The* COLONEL *speaks severely*) This means also for you, Jacobowsky.

JACOBOWSKY

For me? *Twice* for me! I wept when I was born and every day shows me why. (*The* COLONEL *himself stands still for a moment, then takes from the pocket of his tunic a Catholic prayer book and from it reads a prayer in Polish. He intones the words in a liturgical singsong and the sound of them, though strange, conveys somehow the resonant cadence of a great cathedral. He finishes the prayer, puts the prayer book back in his pocket, and in the same voice invokes the future*) I, Tadeusz Boleslav Stjerbinsky, go from Paris not to fly from the Hun but to overthrow him! (*Suddenly relapsing into the vernacular*) All right, push! (*The others resume their pushing with all their strength. The* COLONEL *sits behind the wheel ready to guide the car*) Push! Push! (*They strain and push but the car is rooted to the spot.*)

CHAUFFEUR
(*From the tangle*)
The brake! Release the brake!

MADAME BOUFFIER
Release the brake, you big fool!

COLONEL
(*Bewildered for a moment*)
What? Brake? (*Releases the brake*) Oh, the brake! Push! Forward!

(*Now the car responds. It begins to roll forward.* SZABUNIE-WICZ *and the* CHAUFFEUR *pushing strongly,* JACOBOWSKY *rather more doubtfully.* MADAME BOUFFIER, *beside herself, begins to cry. She waves her handkerchief at* JACOBOWSKY. *He takes time off for a moment to wave back to her.*)

MADAME BOUFFIER
God save Jacobowsky!

Curtain

ACT TWO

ACT TWO

Scene I

Scene: St. Cyrille. A lonely country road running along a garden wall. The wall is broken by a gate; the villa faintly visible through the gate beyond thick trees. Summer dusk. From time to time the roar of German planes.

MARIANNE, a lovely and vivacious young French woman, slim and girlish, is talking to her lawyer, SEROUILLE, a crotchety old man.

SEROUILLE

(Importuning her)

You are young. You are strong. Life is still before you. I implore you—fly, run away, vanish—while there is still time—before the Germans come.

MARIANNE

I am surprised at you, Serouille, talking like that. That is defeatism.

SEROUILLE

It is realism.

MARIANNE

I sent for you to settle my boundary dispute with that pig of a neighbor, not to tell me to run away. Are you my lawyer—or are you hers?

SEROUILLE

Boundary dispute! Six feet of pasture and all rocky.

MARIANNE

But they are my six feet—not hers. I love them, every rock,

59

every pebble. On this land I was born. Here my father and grandfather were born. Here I stay!

(*An airplane zooms rather close. It makes a terrific racket.*)

SEROUILLE
(*Looks up*)

Messerschmitt. Admirable! How undeviating! Know just what they're about.

MARIANNE
(*With hatred*)

They trespass over my beautiful fields. How long will our government allow it? When will they be stopped?

SEROUILLE

Never.

MARIANNE

I am surprised at you, Monsieur Serouille. Can you conceive that France will no longer be France—can you?

SEROUILLE

I cannot conceive it but, alas! I know that it is true.

MARIANNE

But the whole world is with us—the whole world loves France. America! Poland!

SEROUILLE

That love, which so far has not materialized in planes, will not stop the Boches!

MARIANNE

How can you say that! The Poles—look how they fought!

SEROUILLE

But what good was it? The Poles they were done for six months ago. The Germans are a very few miles to the north. What are you waiting for?

MARIANNE

Right now I am waiting for the return of my lover—a noble Pole—Colonel Tadeusz Boleslav Stjerbinsky. Isn't it a lovely name?

SEROUILLE
(*Shakes his head*)

He will not return.

MARIANNE

He will! Moreover he will return with men, with planes, with guns. He did not go to Paris for nothing.

SEROUILLE

I see there is nothing I can do.

MARIANNE

You can do what I engaged you to do. You can get me back that piece of land from that ugly, thieving Madame Vauclain.

SEROUILLE
(*With a little laugh*)

In forty-eight hours at most your land and her land will both belong to the Germans. Do you think the Boches will insist on a clear title? They are not so meticulous.

MARIANNE

When our deliverance comes I shall not remind you that you have talked like this.

SEROUILLE
(*Turns to go*)

I have done what I could.

MARIANNE
(*Calls after him*)

And tell Vauclain if she goes to court it is she who will have to pay the costs!

SEROUILLE
(*Wearily*)

I'll tell her.

MARIANNE

That'll teach her—the pennypincher!

SEROUILLE

Yes. The world loves us. But the Nazis—*they* covet us! (*He goes out.*)

(*Left alone,* MARIANNE *stands dreamily looking out at her beloved fields, whitening in the bright moonlight. She is deeply stirred. Involuntarily her lips pronounce her lover's name. She hears herself murmuring.*)

MARIANNE

Colonel Tadeusz Boleslav Stjerbinsky—Lover, Deliverer . . . (*She becomes conscious that she is saying it and then she speaks aloud in a firm tone*) Deliverer . . . (*She is in an entranced mood. The barking of her little dog breaks her out of it.*) Oh, Coco! (*She runs through the gate and disappears in the garden.*)

(*For a second the scene is empty, only the disconsolate peep-peep of crickets audible. Gradually we hear the reluctant pounding and thrashing of an exhausted automobile motor. The sputtering approach can be followed as it comes closer and at last* JACOBOWSKY'S *limousine appears, mud-bespattered, rattling, inching in by jerks. It runs into a heap of stones put up as a tank-obstruction. The car, its right to live impaired, halts with a sharp bump, the doors fly open. The first to tumble out is* JACOBOWSKY. SZABUNIEWICZ *hurries around and looks at the freshly smashed mudguard. The* COLONEL, *tall and leisurely, stands looking around with satisfaction.*)

COLONEL

We arrive!

JACOBOWSKY
(*Rather short-tempered*)

Yes. But where?

COLONEL
(*Grandiose*)

At the object of my heart's desire.

JACOBOWSKY

Also twelve hours nearer the Germans!

SZABUNIEWICZ
(*Tapping the fender*)

Run into French tank-obstruction. Is enough to make laugh the Germans.

JACOBOWSKY

Are we running away from the Germans or do we have a rendezvous with them? Colonel, you will never know what these twelve hours have cost me!

COLONEL
(*Fixes him with a blue-eyed military stare*)

Cost you? Polish Government pay you back everything. Szabuniewicz, child, write down everything what we owe this *merchant*. Myself I have no head for figures.

SZABUNIEWICZ

Figures leave to me . . .

COLONEL

Therefore every time write down. Everything write down.

SZABUNIEWICZ
(*Taps his forehead*)

In my head is written!

COLONEL

Therefore, Polish Government, what it owe him?

JACOBOWSKY

Write down in your head the Polish Government in Exile owes me the following: Replacement One: a heart which has begun to flutter like a wounded bird; Replacement Two: one wrecked nervous system, plus body ditto. And, if the Germans catch me, one entire Jacobowsky.

COLONEL

(*Gruffly, drowning all in the computable*)
Szabuniewicz, what costs him this car?

SZABUNIEWICZ

Seventeen thousand francs.

COLONEL

Therefore for the car put down twenty thousand francs. Ten thousand add for gasoline and other slight specialties what we use. Also five thousand for two rugs was left behind.

SZABUNIEWICZ

Polish Government owe him now thirty-five thousand francs!

COLONEL

(*Haughtily*)
Now hear me, S. L. Jacobowsky! For this amount thirty-five thousand we toss the coin! Double or nothing. Give me coin! Top I win. Bottom you win. (*Takes coin from* JACOBOWSKY. *He tosses it into his palm, and reaches out his palm for* SZABUNIEWICZ *to register the result.* SZABUNIEWICZ *looks at coin and pockets it.*)

SZABUNIEWICZ

Polish Government owe him now seventy thousand francs.

COLONEL
(*Lavishly*)

Write down!

SZABUNIEWICZ
(*Tapping his brow*)

Is written.

JACOBOWSKY
(*Looks up*)

Why—will you please tell me—why are we getting ourselves involved in all these intricate financial transactions when every second the Germans are getting closer?

COLONEL
(*Scornful*)

You are in a hurry it seem.

(SZABUNIEWICZ *fishes out from the car a cigar box containing the* COLONEL's *toilet articles.*)

JACOBOWSKY

And you are not in a hurry? This Messiah in the gray gloves who is waiting to save you in St. Jean de Luz is not in a hurry? That corvette filled with Czechs and Poles is not in a hurry?

(SZABUNIEWICZ *is brushing the* COLONEL's *uniform.*)

COLONEL

This corvette for us—not for you.

JACOBOWSKY

I know. But I want a sight of the ocean. Perhaps for me, too, a Moses will appear and will divide the Channel and let me walk across to England.

(SZABUNIEWICZ *starts polishing the* COLONEL's *boots.*)

COLONEL

Szabuniewicz, how many hours before our appointment at St. Jean de Luz?

SZABUNIEWICZ
(*Polishing away*)

Seventy-two.

COLONEL

Ample.

JACOBOWSKY

You don't think of breakdowns, the eternal problem of gasoline.

COLONEL

Is in your blood to get gasoline.

JACOBOWSKY

Colonel, I don't understand you. Really—I don't understand you. You seem to look down on the instinct of self-preservation.

COLONEL

In your case this ambition is trivial. (*He looks at* SZABUNIEWICZ *to get appreciation for his little joke.* SZABUNIEWICZ *responds. They both laugh.* SZABUNIEWICZ *hands the* COLONEL *a comb and holds a mirror while the* COLONEL *combs his hair.*) You do not realize that I, Stjerbinsky, under greater danger than little Jacobowsky. On my head the Germans have put price! (*He returns the comb to* SZABUNIEWICZ.)

JACOBOWSKY

At the rate you're going, they'll collect it! Is this a time to stop for ladies?

COLONEL

Life of man is short but always time to think of ladies. For my spirit—this is the fuel. Without this fuel, I can no more live than this car without gasoline.

(SZABUNIEWICZ *gets perfume bottle from cigar box.*)

JACOBOWSKY
(*Throws up his hands*)

Reason rebels!

COLONEL

Reason always rebel against life. What is reason? A dried-up little bureaucrat with a green eye-shade. . . . (*Pointing to* MARI-ANNE's *house*) To that lady the Colonel give his word to return. I am return! Of equal importance my mission and my word. But this of course you don't understand. The concept of honor is not for you.

(SZABUNIEWICZ *dabs perfume on* COLONEL's *hands.*)

SZABUNIEWICZ

Promise of Spring.
(*The* COLONEL *inhales the scent with satisfaction.*)

JACOBOWSKY

Isn't your concept of honor a little exclusive? Like a private park with a "No Trespass Sign," don't you think?

COLONEL

I do not think. I feel. I act. Food—I eat. Gun—I shoot. Horse —I ride. Woman—I love. Honor—I defend.

JACOBOWSKY

Admirable. A Renaissance figure as sure as the world is round.

COLONEL
(*Leans on car. Truculent*)

Who say that?

JACOBOWSKY

Who says what?

COLONEL
(*Ready to make a fight for it*)

That she's round!

JACOBOWSKY

I don't insist. There is no doubt, Colonel, you have one of the finest minds of the fifteenth century. Unfortunately I live in the twentieth. I implore you, Colonel, see your lady and let's go.

SZABUNIEWICZ
(*Looking toward the house*)

Windows is dark . . .

COLONEL

Mademoiselle is sleeping probably.

SZABUNIEWICZ

I go knock.

JACOBOWSKY

Blow the horn.

COLONEL

(*Indignant*)

You wake lady with automobile horn? I break your hands for that! Szabuniewicz, child, my violin is in the car. Mademoiselle is sleeping. We wake her. We wake her sweet.

(SZABUNIEWICZ *has opened the violin case. The* COLONEL *takes the violin with a flourish.* SZABUNIEWICZ *puts the case back in the car.*)

JACOBOWSKY

(*Unable to believe what he sees, fascinated*)

You pick this moment for a recital? (*As* SZABUNIEWICZ *takes a mouth organ out of his pocket and sits on the running board of the car and starts playing scales*) A regular orchestra!

SZABUNIEWICZ

(*Blinking his eyes like a coquette*)

Sir, you not musical?

JACOBOWSKY

In Munich we had chamber music every Wednesday night. I played second fiddle.

COLONEL

You always play second fiddle.

JACOBOWSKY

What's wrong with second? You need as much technique as to play first! Only I didn't have it!

COLONEL

(*Holds his violin lovingly*)

On all the fronts she has been my companion.

JACOBOWSKY

Powerful instrument in the war of nerves. (COLONEL *beats time for* SZABUNIEWICZ *with his bow and then, his back to the audience, facing the house of his beloved, he goes into Drigo's "Sere-*

nade" while SZABUNIEWICZ *accompanies him on the mouth organ.*
All of this JACOBOWSKY *watches incredulously. He presses his*
knuckles to his temples) Is this real? The air is filled with
German planes. The earth is crimson. Poland lies slain—and this
last of her dead stands here fiddling in the moonlight! And I,
the only son of Reba Jacobowsky, am lost, far from home, motor-
ing to the guillotine in Rothschild's limousine! It is a grotesque
dream I dream. . . .

> (*In the misty distance,* MARIANNE *appears. The* COLONEL
> *hands his violin to* SZABUNIEWICZ; *calls as if over an im-*
> *measurable distance.*)

COLONEL

Marianne. . . .

MARIANNE
(Answers)

Tadeusz. . . .

COLONEL

I am return. . . .

MARIANNE

I am here. . . .

COLONEL

My arms wait to receive you. . . .
> (*By this time* MARIANNE *has come running through the*
> *garden gate into the* COLONEL'S *arms.*)

MARIANNE

I knew you would come back. I never faltered.

COLONEL
(Enjoying himself hugely)

My journey is over. (*He kisses her*) My journey begins.

MARIANNE

Tadeusz.

COLONEL

My loved one.
(*They embrace.*)

MARIANNE

I fell asleep just now—I dreamt you were here—with guns, with planes—driving the Boches away.
(SZABUNIEWICZ *is playing a lively tune on the harmonica.*)

COLONEL
(*Grimly*)

This I greatly fear was only a . . . (*Wrathfully to* SZABUNIE-WICZ) Stop damn all to hell this music! (SZABUNIEWICZ *obeys despondently. He is more hurt than angry. The* COLONEL *resumes his aria*) That, I fear, was only a dream.

MARIANNE
(*Sees plaster on* COLONEL's *forehead*)

But, darling! You are wounded. What did they do to you?

COLONEL

I no longer fight the Boches. I run from them. And you run with me.

MARIANNE
(*Aghast*)

Run!

COLONEL

We must. To Bordeaux. To London!

MARIANNE

Then it's true. France is defeated.

COLONEL

For the moment.

MARIANNE

Everybody said it. And now you say it. You too!

COLONEL

I say it too!

MARIANNE
(*Dead voice*)

Then it must be true. If you abandon us too—then it must be true. (*It takes a moment for her to assimilate this awful fact*) France—France is . . . (SZABUNIEWICZ *steps forward to arrange something in back of car.* MARIANNE *sees him*) Oh! Szabuniewicz . . .

SZABUNIEWICZ

At your service, honored lady.

MARIANNE
(*Sees* JACOBOWSKY)

Who is that?

COLONEL

Not to be frightened, my life. It is only S. L. Jacobowsky.

JACOBOWSKY

The modest owner of this car, which bears us all to safety.

COLONEL
(*Stern*)

You forget, Jacobowsky. This car requisition by Polish Government. And pay you well for it. (*To* MARIANNE) But very obliging person, my love. Takes care of everything—car, hotel rooms, *marrons glacés,* gasoline. What you will, Jacobowsky provides. Jacobowsky, gasoline! See?

JACOBOWSKY

Gasoline. It's easy to say. A pipeline to the sky.

COLONEL

If necessary.

JACOBOWSKY

Unfortunately, at the moment, the sky is in the possession of the Nazis!

COLONEL

Marianne, please to go and pack. Szabuniewicz and I—we help you.

MARIANNE

No, Tadeusz, my love.

COLONEL

No?

MARIANNE

I cannot leave.

COLONEL

But you must.

MARIANNE

I have never left France. I never shall.

COLONEL

But I ask you. I demand. It is necessary we do not part.

MARIANNE

We must. I love you. But to leave this land, I cannot do this.

COLONEL

I leave my land.

MARIANNE

I know. Other people do it. They leave their countries lightly. I cannot go. Go without me.

(JACOBOWSKY *intervenes, taps* COLONEL *on shoulder.*)

COLONEL

What you want?

JACOBOWSKY

I overheard your discussion.

COLONEL

Always you eavesdrop!

JACOBOWSKY
(*To* MARIANNE)

The Colonel is a peculiar man. When he shouts to me and I answer, he says I eavesdrop. (MARIANNE *smiles*) Madame, if I may make so bold, there are times when in order to advance one must retreat. This is one of those times.

MARIANNE

I cannot run away.

JACOBOWSKY

Right now the shortest distance between this gate—and that house—is Bordeaux, London and back. Please believe me, Madame.

MARIANNE

Is it so hopeless?

JACOBOWSKY

For the moment. I am a subtle man, and I have read much, but the Colonel here has a faculty worth more than all my subtleties. He will escape with you, but he will also return with you and he will fight for you.

COLONEL

I do not need you to speak for me, Monsieur.

JACOBOWSKY
(*Briskly*)

It will save time. You have the same idea I have but it takes you too long to gather your thoughts.

COLONEL
(*Storms*)

I will not permit you to . . .

JACOBOWSKY
(*To* MARIANNE)

To come back here he risked his life.

MARIANNE
(*Looks up at* COLONEL *gratefully*)

Tadeusz . . .

JACOBOWSKY
What's more, he risked mine. Did we do that for nothing? Abandon your home, Madame, in order to save your home.

MARIANNE
You are returning to fight for France again?

JACOBOWSKY
Not I. He.

COLONEL
(*To be just for once*)
He is not a soldier, Marianne!

JACOBOWSKY
I fight in my own way. Here I am a superfluous man, but even a superfluous man wants to go on being superfluous. Please, Madame, make up your mind. Hurry! Join us.

MARIANNE
(*Amused, to* COLONEL)
Your friend is funny.

COLONEL
He is a traveling acquaintance, merely.

MARIANNE
But amusing and sympathetic!

JACOBOWSKY
Madame, every minute counts.

MARIANNE
(*To* COLONEL)
You will bring me back?

COLONEL
I will bring you back.
(*They kiss.*)

MARIANNE
(*In a flurry*)

Coco and Mignon are in their baskets. They are very frightened. I've got to shut off the gas and water. I've got to pack my things. Tadeusz, will you help me?

COLONEL

Szabuniewicz and I—we both help you!

JACOBOWSKY
(*Adores her already*)

I'll help you, too . . .

COLONEL

Mademoiselle has protector. You get gasoline.

MARIANNE
(*As she goes out through the gate*)

If he gets gasoline, that's wonderful help. (*To* JACOBOWSKY) Good luck! (*She hurries out, followed by* STJERBINSKY *and* SZABUNIEWICZ.)

COLONEL
(*As he and* SZABUNIEWICZ *follow her*)

Fill up the tank!
(*Left alone, with his chore,* JACOBOWSKY *sighs.*)

JACOBOWSKY
(*Murmurs to himself*)

Fill up the tank! Easy to say! Pipeline to the sky! (*He does a little turn by himself in the moonlight, his hands in his pockets, whistling "La Donna è Mobile." Suddenly a plane returns not far away and starts spitting machine-gun bullets.* JACOBOWSKY *jumps into the back of the car; obeying some reflex, though the top is down and he is exposed to the heavens, he bends, pulling his coat collar over his head. The plane recedes. Cautiously he straightens up, feeling his body all over. He has not observed the entrance of a* BRIGADIER *of the Gendarmerie on a bicycle.*)

Now the BRIGADIER *dismounts. He wears a red cap and service pouch.*)

JACOBOWSKY
(*Very friendly, to the* BRIGADIER)

Good evening.

BRIGADIER
(*Businesslike*)

Good evening. Your identification, please.
    (JACOBOWSKY *gets out of the car, starts fishing out his documents, and hands the paper to* BRIGADIER.)

JACOBOWSKY
(*Sighs*)

Ah! The one fate you can't escape—your own identity.

BRIGADIER
(*More politely*)

Literary man?

JACOBOWSKY

Only as a lover. Not a practitioner.

BRIGADIER

Your safe-conduct pass, please.

JACOBOWSKY
(*Mastering his anxiety*)

Safe-conduct pass?

BRIGADIER

As a foreigner you have no right to fluctuate freely without the proper authorization.

JACOBOWSKY
(*Dryly*)

But I'm fluctuating under compulsion, not freely. All of France is fluctuating now.

BRIGADIER

To be more specific, what are your personal plans, Monsieur?

JACOBOWSKY

My personal plans are so fluid I'm apt to drown in them.

BRIGADIER

(*Rattling off the rigmarole—tapping papers*)

This paper gives your basic place of residence as Paris. If you desire to change your basic place of residence, you are required to submit to the Commissariat of Police of your precinct an application for stamped forms wherein you request the privilege of changing your residence. The Commissariat of Police will transmit your application to the Prefecture, which, after careful investigation and examination, will forward it to the Central Military Bureau of Circulation who will then decide in accordance with the prevailing situation in regard to transportation and communication whether you have the right to move to this spot to which you have already moved.

JACOBOWSKY

Sergeant, tell me—has the rumor by any chance reached you that Paris is about to fall to the Germans?

BRIGADIER

When it happens, that will be a mere fact. It will not alter the provisions of the law. You are accordingly required to proceed forthwith to Paris, Monsieur, and follow the legally prescribed course. Otherwise you are illegally, illicitly and surreptitiously standing on this highway. You are standing before me only de facto, not de jure.

JACOBOWSKY

That means arrest and shipping off to Paris?

BRIGADIER

In accordance with the regulations.

JACOBOWSKY

You know what the Boches will do with me if they catch me?

BRIGADIER

They won't eat you.

JACOBOWSKY

Especially me. For them I am caviar!

BRIGADIER

If they do execute you, at least you will have the satisfaction of knowing that you have not broken the regulations of France.

JACOBOWSKY

I shall die happy.

BRIGADIER

With a clear conscience. A good way to die . . .

JACOBOWSKY

Tell me, sir, unofficially . . .

BRIGADIER

I cannot give you an *un*official answer until nine o'clock, when I shall be off duty . . .

JACOBOWSKY
(*Looks at his watch*)

Three to nine. What I was going to ask was . . . Officer, I have an irresistible compulsion to leave the soil of France. How should I go about it?

BRIGADIER

For the purpose of leaving France you require a visa de sortie. For this purpose you must apply to the nearest Sous-Prefecture, at Sable d'Olonnes, for such a visa de sortie, first executing three questionnaires, each with one photograph, profile, showing right ear, and paying a fee of twenty-seven francs, seventy-five centimes. The Sous-Prefecture will communicate with the Prefecture of your basic place of residence, Paris, and will, by extended correspondence, compile a dossier of your case, which, after a few weeks, will be submitted to the Ministry of the Interior for further action. (*They consult their watches*) The Ministry of the

Interior instructs a special commission to investigate whether you were worthy to set foot on French soil, and whether you are worthy to leave it. That takes a certain amount of time, but goes through with the greatest smoothness. There is, however, difficulty in your case. You must first return to Paris, and await your safe-conduct pass, permitting you to come here. Is that clear?

JACOBOWSKY

Crystal!

BRIGADIER

Monsieur is very intelligent. However, I must frankly tell you that even if you fulfill all the requirements I have just enumerated, your prospects are nil. After all, what consideration can you expect from a government which you have caused so much clerical work? You'd better come along with me right now.

JACOBOWSKY
(*Looks at watch*)

Nine o'clock!

BRIGADIER
(*Greatly relieved*)

Nine? Good—then I'm off duty. (*He and* JACOBOWSKY *both sit on bench, quite relaxed*) Now I can talk to you unofficially.

JACOBOWSKY

What would you do if you were me?

BRIGADIER

You want to go down the coast to Bayonne and beyond. Right?

JACOBOWSKY

Right.

BRIGADIER

Keep away from the shore roads to begin with. They are advancing fast along the coast.

JACOBOWSKY

Thank you very much, but I am unable to follow your counsel.

BRIGADIER

Why?

JACOBOWSKY

I have no gasoline—not a drop.

(MARIANNE *comes in. She has two baskets containing Coco and Mignon. She is surprised to see the* BRIGADIER.)

BRIGADIER

That's a pity.

JACOBOWSKY

Could you help me? Is there . . . ?

BRIGADIER

(*Sees* MARIANNE, *rises*)

Good evening, Mamselle Roualet.

MARIANNE

Oh, good evening. Monsieur Jacobowsky—would you help me?

JACOBOWSKY

(*Goes to her, takes baskets*)

You remember my name?

MARIANNE

Why shouldn't I?

JACOBOWSKY

Some people have difficulty. . . .

MARIANNE

Will you please—Coco and Mignon—they hate leaving home as much as I do.

JACOBOWSKY

I'll make them comfortable. I love animals. They accept you without reservation. (*He puts the baskets carefully in the back of the car.*)

MARIANNE
(*To* BRIGADIER)

This gentleman is taking us off in his car.

BRIGADIER
(*To* JACOBOWSKY)

Why didn't you tell me?

MARIANNE

And a noble Polish officer—who will return one day to fight for France. Do you think it dreadful of me to leave?

BRIGADIER
(*Warmly*)

No, it is good you are going.

JACOBOWSKY
(*Calls across to the* BRIGADIER, *urgently*)

Gasoline—gasoline.

BRIGADIER
(*Stamping document*)

Take this stamped document. My colleague in St. Cyrille will furnish you with thirty gallons at the standard price. (*He hands him the stamped paper.* JACOBOWSKY *takes it.*)

JACOBOWSKY
(*Moved*)

My friend. My dear friend. How is it possible to thank a man like you?

BRIGADIER
(*Gets back on his bicycle. Crisply*)

Carry the greetings of Brigadier Jouet to England and to America.

JACOBOWSKY
(*Fervently*)

I shall. I shall.

BRIGADIER
(*To* MARIANNE)

Mamselle Roualet, I bless you. I bless your journey. I bless your mission.

JACOBOWSKY AND MARIANNE
(*Simultaneously*)

Amen.

BRIGADIER

If I were younger, I would go with you. But all I can do is put stamps on papers. Monsieur, I am happy to have given you what may be my last stamp for France. (*He pedals off into the dark.*)

JACOBOWSKY
(*Overcome*)

You are good fortune, Mademoiselle. You are mercy. You are hope!

MARIANNE

If I thought I would not see these fields again . . .

JACOBOWSKY

You will see them.

MARIANNE
(*Torn*)

My poor country.

JACOBOWSKY

It will be re-born. There will be a new France, a new world —because the old one is sick of its own ineptitude.

MARIANNE

You are a comfort, Monsieur.

JACOBOWSKY

You make me wish for youth that I might return and fight too.

MARIANNE

Thank you, Monsieur.

JACOBOWSKY
(*Involuntarily*)

I shall dedicate myself to you.

MARIANNE
(*Rather amused*)

Thank you, Monsieur.

JACOBOWSKY

And to Coco and to Mignon. Have you any other pets?

MARIANNE

Only the Colonel.

JACOBOWSKY

To him I am already dedicated.

MARIANNE
(*Laughing out loud*)

So am I.

(JACOBOWSKY *joins in her laughter. The* COLONEL *comes in carrying a little hatbox. He is surprised at the rapport there seems to have sprung up between* MARIANNE *and* JACOBOWSKY.)

COLONEL

What you laughing at?

MARIANNE

Nothing.

COLONEL
(*To* JACOBOWSKY)

Why do *you* laugh?

JACOBOWSKY

For no reason.

COLONEL

You get gasoline?

JACOBOWSKY
(*Softly*)

Gasoline came to us.

COLONEL

What does he talk—us?

JACOBOWSKY

A warm rain came down from heaven and behold—it was gasoline.

MARIANNE
(*Sharing his mood*)
Pipeline from the sky!
(*They both laugh again.*)

COLONEL

Now what do you laugh at?

JACOBOWSKY

Nothing.

MARIANNE

Nothing.
(*The* COLONEL *is irritated by their evident sympathy. This irritation breaks out into complaint as* SZABUNIEWICZ, *loaded with* MARIANNE's *bundles, staggers in.*)

COLONEL

Marianne, is not possible take all this stuff.

JACOBOWSKY

Why not?

COLONEL

Because is no room.

JACOBOWSKY

Room is elastic. Room can be made to expand.

COLONEL
(*To* SZABUNIEWICZ)
Less and less I like this Jacobowsky!

SZABUNIEWICZ
(*Echoes*)

Less and less. (*He lifts large bag and is about to throw it into the car.*)

MARIANNE
(*Concerned for her pets*)

Mignon—Coco . . .

JACOBOWSKY
(*Goes over, puts bag in carefully*)

They're in a safe place.

COLONEL
(*Bursts out*)

Not to worry, Marianne. Everyone safe. Dogs safe. You safe. Szabuniewicz safe. I safe. All protect by Monsieur Jacobowsky.

JACOBOWSKY

I do not undertake quite so much, Colonel. Only these little dogs—for them I am Goliath—a miniature Goliath.

(MARIANNE *laughs.*)

COLONEL

What you laugh at?

MARIANNE

I don't know. He makes me laugh. Why are you so bad-tempered?

(SZABUNIEWICZ *has already started packing boxes in the car.*)

COLONEL
(*Roars*)

Marianne, cannot take all those packages!

SZABUNIEWICZ
(*Lifting hatbox*)

He travels light.

JACOBOWSKY

Plenty of room.

MARIANNE

Perhaps we can leave behind one bandbox.

JACOBOWSKY

I wouldn't hear of it. (*He takes hatbox from* SZABUNIEWICZ *and puts it in car.*)

COLONEL
(*Roars at him*)

Who you not to hear of anything?

JACOBOWSKY
(*To* COLONEL)

Let me explain, Colonel. You are a great man but as a refugee I am more experienced. Let me tell you—nothing is so warming to morale in difficult hours as to have a few precious, familiar knickknacks with you. It restores your identity—gives you a link with the past, a bridge to what you were. It's important, believe me, it's important, and especially for a lady.

MARIANNE
(*Drawn to him*)

You are *so understanding,* Monsieur Jacobowsky.
(*The* COLONEL *towers above them while* MARIANNE *and* JACOBOWSKY *talk to each other.*)

JACOBOWSKY
(*To* MARIANNE *under the shadow of this tower*)

It's experience, Mademoiselle, simple experience.
(*They both laugh again.*)

COLONEL
(*Walks between them in a rage*)

All right! Take whole damn business, only let's go. You make of this car a furniture truck.

MARIANNE

We'll compromise. I'll give up this hatbox.
(SZABUNIEWICZ *picks up the tiny hatbox.*)

COLONEL
(*Sarcastic*)

This will be great help!

SZABUNIEWICZ
(*Seized with a bright idea, whispers to* COLONEL)

Colonel, sew papers in little hat.

COLONEL
(*Assimilating the idea slowly*)

What you say?

SZABUNIEWICZ

Hide documents in little hat.

COLONEL
(*Straightens up. Announces pridefully—any idea* SZABUNIE-WICZ *might have belongs to him automatically*)

Attention! I have important idea! We take this bandbox, Marianne. In your little hat you sew my documents. Germans will never look there for them. (*He is very owlish about this.*)

JACOBOWSKY

It is an inspiration!

MARIANNE
(*Bubbling*)

And it will make me feel so important.

COLONEL

Now at last we go! Marianne, the back seat. (*He gets in and sits at the wheel*) Szabuniewicz—beside me.
(SZABUNIEWICZ *complies.*)

MARIANNE
(*Barely fitting into a pile of luggage in the back seat, looks around to* JACOBOWSKY)

It's so crowded here. Where will you sit?

JACOBOWSKY
(*Darting forward*)

With great happiness at your feet. (*He gets in the back of the car, sitting on the floor at* MARIANNE's *feet, his own on the running board.*)

COLONEL
(*Turning from the wheel*)

Szabuniewicz—change places with him.

MARIANNE
(*As* SZABUNIEWICZ *starts to comply; pats* JACOBOWSKY)

No. I like him here. He comforts me.

COLONEL
(*To* SZABUNIEWICZ)

Less and less I like this Jacobowsky.

SZABUNIEWICZ
(*Echoes*)

Less and less.

MARIANNE
(*Consoling* JACOBOWSKY)

Never mind! (*She smiles down at the ravished* JACOBOWSKY, *who looks up at her adoringly.* SZABUNIEWICZ *bangs the front door. The fretting vehicle moves off.*)

Curtain

ACT TWO

Scene II

Scene: *An open spot in the woods near the city of Bayonne. An overcast summer day. In the background on the highway, somewhat elevated, stands* JACOBOWSKY'S *car even more battered than before. In the middle distance a little stream winds through at which passing refugees stop to drink.*

At Rise: *In the foreground on a little slope at the right* MARI-ANNE *sits on a small trunk at the foot of an immense haystack. At her feet is the* COLONEL'S *civilian coat, quite tattered. The* COLONEL *is wearing civvies, corduroy trousers and an old shirt. It is the first time we have seen him without his uniform. Without it he is depressed. In these shabby misfits he feels himself deprived of his identity. He is moodily fighting melancholia.*

When the curtain goes up, MARIANNE *has just finished sewing the* COLONEL'S *papers in her little hat. She holds up the hat, pleased at her own handiwork.*

MARIANNE

There—I've sewn your precious papers in my hat. Who would ever think that in this frivolous little hat are the names of the future saviors of Poland? (*She puts the hat in the hatbox*) And now, I'll finish your poor coat! (*She picks up his coat and sews.*)

COLONEL

Without my uniform—I feel like not a man!

MARIANNE
(*Gently, humoring him*)
Were you never without a uniform before?

89

COLONEL

Never!

MARIANNE

You weren't born in a uniform, were you?

COLONEL

(*Automatically*)

Yes. (*Amending his statement*) My father cavalry officer. My grandfather cavalry officer! We Stjerbinskys always in uniform.

MARIANNE

Even when you were a little boy?

COLONEL

When I am little boy I dress up! Always in my dreams I am in uniform.

MARIANNE

(*With a look at the ragged coat*)

Well, this is a kind of uniform too, isn't it?

COLONEL

These filthy rags?

MARIANNE

There is a time to advance and a time to retreat. . . .

COLONEL

That sounds like Monsieur Jacobowsky.

MARIANNE

What you are wearing now is the uniform of retreat.

COLONEL

Please, I beg you not to quote to me Monsieur Jacobowsky.

MARIANNE

Why not?

COLONEL

Because, if I have to govern myself with his mentality, I rather die.

MARIANNE

Monsieur Jacobowsky says it is easy to die. But to live requires ingenuity. . . . This uniform is part of the ingenuity. (*Patting the mended shoulder*) There! I have just sewed on your epaulettes! Look at this hole—sword thrust! This missing button—a sharpshooter! This lapel—what a fierce hand-to-hand encounter that was! Darling, for this uniform you could dream the most heroic exploits. In so many ways you are still a little boy. Go on dreaming!

COLONEL

I cannot dream myself hero in costume like this.

MARIANNE

We used to have a picture in our bedroom when I was a little girl—the Grande Armée returning through the snows of Russia. They were in rags, poor things. I used to shiver for them. Compared to what they wore this battle-scarred coat (*She holds up the poor garment*) is quite grand. In your uniform you were a symbol, darling. Wonderful, but a symbol. But in this you are a human being. I'm glad for once to have seen you in it. I love you in it.

COLONEL

This also sounds like Monsieur Jacobowsky.

MARIANNE

It's not very flattering of you to assume that I am an echo of Monsieur Jacobowsky. Am I so stupid?

COLONEL

When first I know you you do not talk like this.

MARIANNE

When I first knew you, it was so close and thrilling that, as I recall it, we didn't talk at all. There was no time between kisses.

COLONEL

(*Bitterly*)

But now there is plenty of time!

MARIANNE

Yes. The roads are so crowded—the waits so long, for meals, for a place to sleep, for a drop of gasoline.

COLONEL

And this time mainly you use to talk to Monsieur Jacobowsky!

MARIANNE

Yes. It passes the time.

COLONEL
(*Tensely*)

What you talk about?

MARIANNE

All sorts of things.

COLONEL

Sometimes I come upon you, you stop talking. Sudden you stop.

MARIANNE

Do we?

COLONEL

Why you stop?

MARIANNE

I don't know. I suppose because Monsieur Jacobowsky is afraid you won't be sympathetic or interested.

COLONEL

I don't ask why he stop—I ask why *you* stop.

MARIANNE

Do I?

COLONEL

Yes—you stop.

MARIANNE
(*Facing it*)

I suppose I must feel the same as Monsieur Jacobowsky feels —that you won't be sympathetic or interested.

COLONEL

(The damning evidence is now in his possession. He draws himself up accusingly)

This is how I suspect. You no longer feel like me. You feel like Monsieur Jacobowsky.

MARIANNE

Isn't it possible to feel like you both?

COLONEL

No. Never. Impossible.

MARIANNE
(Laughs)

Darling!

COLONEL

You laugh at me.

MARIANNE

A little. In this hard journey—do you grudge me a little laugh?

COLONEL

But not at me. To this I am not used.

MARIANNE

All right, Tadeusz. If it will make you feel better, I will not laugh any more. There! *(The coat is finished. He puts it on. It hangs on him clumsily. She does her best to make it fit)* Shoulder better?

COLONEL

Shoulder better. Heart wounded!

MARIANNE

Poor heart. Poor heart. I'll mend that too.

COLONEL
(Tragic)

You don't mend. You break.

MARIANNE

Darling, because you catch me talking nonsense with poor little Monsieur Jacobowsky!

COLONEL
(*Fixed idea*)

If nonsense, then why you stop when I come?

MARIANNE

Perhaps it's because you're a hero. Too epic for nonsense.

COLONEL

This also sounds like Monsieur Jacobowsky.

MARIANNE
(*With self-revelation, with surprise*)

Yes, it does! It's just like him!

COLONEL

He loves you, this Monsieur Jacobowsky.

MARIANNE
(*Walks to brook and sits down beside it*)

Ridiculous! What an idea! Do you think so? Perhaps he does —a little bit. Oh! It's touching.

COLONEL

You love him too.

MARIANNE

Now, Tadeusz, don't be silly.

COLONEL

Then what you see in him? Why you like him?

MARIANNE
(*Exploring her own mind*)

Why I like him?

COLONEL

You like him better than me!

MARIANNE
(*Scrupulously honest*)
In one way perhaps.

COLONEL
(*Triumphant*)
Ah, you admit! Why? Why?

MARIANNE
(*Resolute*)
I will tell you why. He makes me more—you make me less.

COLONEL
(*Scientifically*)
I think it necessary I kill this Monsieur Jacobowsky. I fight him.

MARIANNE
You're so absent-minded. You forget it's the Germans you're fighting. (*She wanders back to the trunk at the foot of the hay-stack and sits.*)

COLONEL
Then what you want I do with him? Engage in arguments with him?

MARIANNE
Why not? Good for you.

COLONEL
I do not argue with people like Jacobowsky over the woman I love.

MARIANNE
(*Teasing him*)
Oh, it doesn't have to be about me. You can argue with him over all sorts of subjects—abstract subjects.

COLONEL
You make fun of me. This I do not tolerate.

MARIANNE
What shall I do with you!

COLONEL

Never did I believe that I, Stjerbinsky, would wear costume like this and have for rival S. L. Jacobowsky.

MARIANNE
(*With gusto*)

Both good for you!

COLONEL

Ah! You admit!

MARIANNE

Admit what?

COLONEL

He *is* my rival.

MARIANNE

Not so much your rival, darling, as . . .

COLONEL

As what?

MARIANNE

Your antidote! (*A silence*) The odd thing is, darling, Monsieur Jacobowsky adores you. (*She goes to* COLONEL, *trying to win sympathy for* JACOBOWSKY, *pleading with him, but the* COLONEL's *expression is impassive*) He's constantly telling me how wonderful you are. (*She keeps stealing glances at him but so far no change*) He envies you. He wants you to love him. He wants the whole world to love him.

COLONEL
(*With satisfaction*)

In this he will never succeed.

MARIANNE

He knows that. Don't you find it touching? How cheerful he is. How gentle he is. Don't you find it—appealing? He wants so to be loved. I find it very—very . . .

COLONEL

Obviously you do!

MARIANNE

What shall I do then? Not speak to him? Ignore him? It's his car, after all. We're his guests.

COLONEL

Polish Government pay him in full—with profit.

MARIANNE

Then we're all guests of the Polish Government. Shall I be rude to a fellow guest?
(*The* COLONEL *looks at her. He decides on a new attack.*)

COLONEL

(*He sidles over to her, tries to be light and gay*)
Marianne?

MARIANNE

Yes, my dear.

COLONEL

You and I—why we don't talk about trivial things? Why we don't laugh together?

MARIANNE

(*Moved, but with a gleam. He sits beside her on the trunk*)
I'm willing.

COLONEL

(*Casting about for a delightful subject—finally*)
Do you know something about ballistics?

MARIANNE

Very little, but I'd love to learn.

COLONEL

You know, is very interesting science, ballistics. The trajectory of a cannon ball is a beautiful thing. My father used to draw me pictures when I am a boy of the trajectory the cannon balls make through space. He drew with different colored chalks. Like a rainbow they looked.

MARIANNE
(*Solemnly appreciative*)

It must have been beautiful.

COLONEL
(*Dejected*)

No good!

MARIANNE
(*Looks up at him*)

What?

COLONEL

This subject, ballistics, not trivial enough.

MARIANNE

Let's try something else.
(*Pause.*)

COLONEL

My great-great-great-grandmother when Napoleon came to Poland danced with him in Grand Ball in Warsaw.

MARIANNE

Was she beautiful?

COLONEL

Very beautiful. She danced with Napoleon!

MARIANNE

That's very interesting.

COLONEL

It's history.
(*Pause.*)

MARIANNE

Have you her picture?

COLONEL
(*Wandering—he has a sense of defeat*)

Whose picture?

MARIANNE

Your grandmother's.

COLONEL

Oh, yes. In my home in Poland—but that home probably now destroyed by the Germans.

MARIANNE
(*Sadly*)

Like all our homes.

COLONEL

Damn to hell. This subject is too tragic. It does not make you laugh like Monsieur Jacobowsky.

MARIANNE

Oh, darling, don't try to be like Monsieur Jacobowsky. You have your style—he has his. I love you both.

COLONEL
(*Smarting with a sense of defeat and snapping back to his own identity, rises*)

My course is clear. We fight.

MARIANNE

Oh, my God!

COLONEL

No way out. We fight.

MARIANNE
(*Worried, rises*)

Have you no other way of coping with a situation than to fight?

COLONEL

For a man of honor is no other way.

MARIANNE

I wish, in addition to being a man of honor . . .

COLONEL
(*Sharp*)

Is not enough for you?

MARIANNE

I wish you had a little humor.

COLONEL

When I love I do not laugh.

MARIANNE

We French do. We manage both very well. Please, Tadeusz, be a darling and get off your high horse. Shake out of the stiff corset of your code. Relax a bit and admit the human race.

COLONEL
(*Worked up more and more*)

This idea you also get from Jacobowsky!

MARIANNE
(*Furious, stamps her foot*)

Don't keep saying that! I knew the alphabet before I met you *or* Monsieur Jacobowsky. You don't know me at all. What makes you think you know anything about me?

COLONEL

I realize now this ignorance. Monsieur Jacobowsky—he make me realize . . .

MARIANNE

Then you should be grateful to him.

COLONEL

I am. I will show my gratitude by allowing him to engage me on the field of honor.

MARIANNE

The field of honor! It's quite true—you're a medieval man, Tadeusz. (COLONEL *opens his mouth for the refrain but she beats him to it, shouting*) Yes, that idea I got from Monsieur Jacobowsky! (*They glare at each other, openly hostile.*)

(SZABUNIEWICZ *limps on dejectedly. He has been walking for quite a while. He leans against the haystack, exhausted, taking off his shoes meanwhile.*)

SZABUNIEWICZ

Is no food—nothing!

COLONEL

(*Working off his anger on* SZABUNIEWICZ, *shouts at him*) I promise Madame you bring to eat, you!

SZABUNIEWICZ

In Bayonne city not even room to walk! All streets is full opp wid autos, wid no gasoline, like us. All hotel and café full opp. And the prices! The shops is wiped clean.

(*Some refugees drift by, loaded with bags and bundles. The* OLD MAN *and the* LITTLE BOY *we have seen before stop at the brook. The* OLD MAN *fills a cup and gives the* LITTLE BOY *a drink.*)

MARIANNE

I'm so hungry! Well, so is all France. (*Watching the refugees as they walk down the road*) Where are they going? They walk, but where do they go?

COLONEL

(*To* SZABUNIEWICZ)

Where is this Jacobowsky? You go forage with him. Where is he?

SZABUNIEWICZ

I look around—he is gone. (*Cocking one eye at the sky*) Soon it rain. My corn fall off with walking. I go in car and sleep.

COLONEL

You only good to sleep, you!

SZABUNIEWICZ

Good we all sleep! Dream we eat maybe! (*He waddles off toward the car, curls up on back seat and goes to sleep.*)

(*Between the* COLONEL *and* MARIANNE *a moody pause. It is a bad moment. The* COLONEL *sits on the trunk.*)

COLONEL

(*Out of his despair*)

Anything I endure but that you do not love me. This I cannot.

MARIANNE

(*Goes and kneels by* COLONEL)

Oh, I do love you, Tadeusz. It is only for you and with you that I would leave France for even one hour.

COLONEL

(*Straightens up*)

Then I am able for anything. (*He kisses her*) My melancholy vanish like mist before the sun. (*He gets up, lifting her up with him.*)

MARIANNE

There's no reason in the world for you to be sad. Be happy. Be happy in my love. (*She embraces him.*)

COLONEL

(*Beams at her*)

I struggle for you. I fight for you. I move mountains for you.

MARIANNE

And will you also be good to poor Monsieur Jacobowsky for me?

COLONEL

(*His hands clench*)

For you—yes.

MARIANNE

You give up this silly notion of fighting him?

COLONEL

For you—yes.

MARIANNE

That's my dear boy. (*She embraces and kisses* COLONEL.)

JACOBOWSKY

(*Breezes in; he is very gay*)

Hello!

COLONEL

(*Annoyed that the moment of his reconciliation should be broken into*)

Is here possible no privacy?

JACOBOWSKY

(*He is lugging a bulging straw shopping bag. He is beaming*)

I met my brother-in-law's cousin! Would you think it—in Bayonne!

MARIANNE

(*To* COLONEL, *smiling*)

His family connections are something fabulous!

JACOBOWSKY

He used to be a conductor of the Gewandhaus Orchestra in Leipzig. Now he's a headwaiter in the leading café in Bayonne. He introduced me to the proprietor—and the proprietor—for a price—let me have some very interesting commodities. (*Shows bag.*)

MARIANNE

(*Ecstatic*)

Food!

COLONEL

(*Resentful at* JACOBOWSKY'S *success*)

You got something to eat?

JACOBOWSKY

Special. Very special. (*He holds up a chop*) For Coco!

MARIANNE

You remembered Coco!

JACOBOWSKY

As you love Coco—I love Coco. (*Gives her the chop.*)

COLONEL

You have large heart it seems!

JACOBOWSKY

Now, Colonel, will you spread out that shawl and we will
create the atmosphere of a picnic? (*Muttering to himself, the*
COLONEL *picks up a rolled rug that is lying in the grass and gives
it to* MARIANNE. *She spreads it out.* JACOBOWSKY *throws down his
hat and overcoat, inadvertently throwing his coat over* MARI-
ANNE'S *hatbox.* MARIANNE *sits on the shawl,* JACOBOWSKY *on the
trunk, taking packages out of bag*) Just as I was walking out of
the café after being told there was nothing, there he was—my
brother-in-law's cousin. He fell on my neck and I fell on his. At
home I never liked him. I hated his conducting. I once said: "He
doesn't understand Mozart no more than a headwaiter," and
look, now he *is* a headwaiter!

MARIANNE
(*Gaily*)

Tadeusz, give Coco her little chop, will you?
(*The* COLONEL, *struggling to control himself, obeys. He
takes the chop from her gingerly and goes back with it to
the car.* JACOBOWSKY *keeps handing edibles to* MARIANNE,
who spreads them on the blanket.)

JACOBOWSKY
(*As he puts them down one by one, he apostrophizes the
delicacies*)

These, my dear Sigismund—that's my brother-in-law's cousin
—this loaf of bread fresh from the oven—erases the memory of
your *Don Giovanni* which you played like a pig.

(*By this time the* COLONEL *has reached the car and waked up* SZABUNIEWICZ.)

SZABUNIEWICZ
(*Grunting*)
What for you don't let me sleep?

COLONEL
I don't sleep, you don't sleep.

SZABUNIEWICZ
Go way, let me sleep.

JACOBOWSKY
(*Picking up pastry box*)
And these crisp brioches—your *Figaro*—which was even worse.
Ah, Marianne, the God of War transmutes a bad conductor into
a perfect headwaiter. Mars has a knack for vocational guidance.
(MARIANNE *laughs.*)

MARIANNE
And you, Monsieur Jacobowsky, what has Mars done for you?

JACOBOWSKY
He introduced me to you. Without him I should never have
known you.

MARIANNE
That's a high price!

JACOBOWSKY
It's a bargain counter. I'd rather be in France escaping with
you than getting a big welcome-home reception anywhere else.
(*They become aware that the* COLONEL *has returned and
is lowering over them. They freeze up suddenly.*)

MARIANNE
Oh, but . . .

COLONEL
Why do you stop talking?

MARIANNE

We don't.

COLONEL

You do. What were you saying, Monsieur Jacobowsky?

JACOBOWSKY
(*Blushing a little*)

I don't remember.

COLONEL
(*Menacing*)

You don't remember!

JACOBOWSKY

It was nothing at all.

COLONEL
(*To* MARIANNE)

Marianne, what was he saying?

MARIANNE

It was nothing at all.

COLONEL

If it nothing at all why you don't go on saying nothing at all?

JACOBOWSKY

Before a man like you, savior of countries, we can't be trivial.

COLONEL

This explanation is not satisfactory. (*He confronts him, menacing.*)

MARIANNE
(*Scared*)

Tadeusz!

JACOBOWSKY
(*Taking bottle from bag*)

Oh! I suppose you thought, Colonel, that I had forgotten you.
Not at all. I thought you'd like this fine cognac. . . . (*Presents him with a bottle of cognac.*)

COLONEL
(*Looking at it*)
1912—bad year. (*Gives* JACOBOWSKY *the bottle.*)
(SZABUNIEWICZ *rouses himself and gets out of car.*)

JACOBOWSKY
(*Takes bottle back*)
A bad year but a good bottle. Sigismund tried it. (*Smiles*)
May I pour for you? (*He is about to pour the brandy into a paper cup when the* COLONEL *stops him.*)

COLONEL
(*Growling*)
Not from paper cup.   Szabuniewicz, my silver cup. (*Takes bottle; to* JACOBOWSKY) You drink from paper cup. All right for you!

JACOBOWSKY
Today I'm drinking water. . . . (*He goes to the brook.*)

MARIANNE
Some water for me, too, please. I'm thirsty. . . .
(JACOBOWSKY *brings* MARIANNE *a drink of water.*)

SZABUNIEWICZ
(*Gives silver cup to* COLONEL; *sees the banquet*)
Who give eat? (*He makes for the food.*)

JACOBOWSKY
Help yourself, my friend.

MARIANNE
I'll make a sandwich for you, Tadeusz. . . .

COLONEL
(*Drinking*)
I not have hunger. . . .

SZABUNIEWICZ
(*Picking up dried fish*)
Women and fish best in the middle.

COLONEL
(*Kicks him*)
Szabuniewicz, not to be impertinent. Don't forget your place.

SZABUNIEWICZ
(*In full mutiny*)
When you not in uniform I man like you and I make jokes like anybody else—huh! (*He backs away before the menacing* COLONEL *and sits on a little embankment upstage, eating hard-boiled eggs.*)

COLONEL
(*Swallowing more cognac*)
Marianne, I apologize for this lout.

JACOBOWSKY
Don't drink too much, Colonel. Please.

COLONEL
(*Indignant*)
Who you to speak to me this way?

JACOBOWSKY
If you put out the candle, Chauffeur, we'll all be in the dark.

COLONEL
(*Swallows again*)
You got gasoline in pocket too?

JACOBOWSKY
I'm working on the problem.

COLONEL
Polish Government now owe you six hundred thousand francs. Double or nothing you not get gasoline today!

JACOBOWSKY
(*Trying to conciliate him with food*)
Try one of these hard-boiled eggs, my friend.

COLONEL
(*His suppressed anger mounting*)
Jacobowsky, I resent you drink water.

JACOBOWSKY
Is that all about me you resent?

COLONEL
No!

MARIANNE
Tadeusz, please stop this!

COLONEL
Stop what . . . ?

MARIANNE
You owe Monsieur an apology!

COLONEL
I owe him!

MARIANNE
Yes, you do. I don't want any more nonsense about Monsieur Jacobowsky. Many women I am telling you would be very lucky to get him—especially in times like these!

COLONEL
(*Drawing himself up full*)
Very well. This so desirable gentleman—I challenge you!

JACOBOWSKY
(*Startled*)
Challenge!

COLONEL
Yes!

JACOBOWSKY
To what?

COLONEL
To a duel. To fight.

JACOBOWSKY

What for? (*Instinctively he draws to* MARIANNE *and she to him. He takes her hand in his.*)

COLONEL
(*Enraged*)

Szabuniewicz—the pistols. (*To* JACOBOWSKY) Take your hand away from her!

MARIANNE
(*Holding onto* JACOBOWSKY's *hand*)

Not while you threaten!

COLONEL
(*To* JACOBOWSKY)

Seducer by sobriety! Other men I can out-drink, out-fight— what I do with you?

JACOBOWSKY

Marianne, I should go away.

MARIANNE
(*Stamps her foot*)

I won't have this—you hear—I won't have it!

JACOBOWSKY

I have felt it coming. We must part.

COLONEL

No. We do not part. (*He drinks more cognac.*)

JACOBOWSKY

He doesn't want me to stay—he doesn't want me to go!

SZABUNIEWICZ

It is the cognac. Colonel always melancholy when he drink!

COLONEL
(*Storms*)

Silence!

(*The outburst is so tremendous that* SZABUNIEWICZ *chokes over his egg.*)

SZABUNIEWICZ
(*Still choking*)

Swallop opp whole egg!

MARIANNE
Tadeusz, what's the matter?

COLONEL
Cognac make a man to see more clear. Jacobowsky, you afraid of me?

JACOBOWSKY
Yes. (*Turns to* MARIANNE) I heard in Bayonne the armistice has been signed in Wiesbaden. The Germans are going to occupy most of France. We have to think of gasoline, how to get to the coast. (*He sits on the trunk.*)

COLONEL
Why do you fear me?

MARIANNE
(*Really frightened now*)

Tadeusz, what's come over you?

(MARIANNE *stares at the* COLONEL *hypnotized.* JACOBOWSKY *keeps looking from one to the other of these two suddenly strange people.*)

COLONEL
(*In a spasm of self-revelation*)

He say, this Jacobowsky, he is afraid of me. I tell you truth— I am afraid of him.

JACOBOWSKY
(*Murmurs*)

Thank you for the compliment!

COLONEL
(*Whirls on him*)

Yes. I, Stjerbinsky, who have fought the Nazis on the Pruth

and on the Somme and on the Vistula, I who have never known fear—now I know fear. I'm afraid of you, Jacobowsky. I am afraid of the thoughts you have that you make her share, the laughter that dries up when I approach. I am afraid of the silence you make between me and Marianne. Talk against you I cannot. But fight you I can. Fight you I must. To prove to myself that I do not fear, I fight. Because if I fear, I die.

JACOBOWSKY

But to prove this to yourself probably I'll have to die.

COLONEL

Perhaps you kill me, why not?

JACOBOWSKY

Why not? Then who will drive the car?

COLONEL
(*Shouts*)

You are too practical!

JACOBOWSKY
(*To* MARIANNE)

Too practical! That's the trouble, Marianne, he is a fifteenth-century man but, unfortunately, I live in the twentieth.

COLONEL
(*Growls*)

Twentieth century I do not like.

JACOBOWSKY

I don't like it either, but what can we do about it?

COLONEL

In twentieth century no poetry, no heroism, no honor. Twentieth century full with fleas and disinfectant, disinfectant and fleas. Everything sanitary, sterilized! Small rooms, good cheap manufacture, mouth wash, chromium fixture, umbrellas and those stuff! Everything in this damn century got to have sense!

But where is style? Who gives elegance? These things I see no more! What is modern is small. You are small man, Jacobowsky. By fighting you I give you stature. What Nazis take away from you, I, Stjerbinsky, give you back—honor!

(JACOBOWSKY *rises*.)

MARIANNE

Tadeusz, you're crazy.

SZABUNIEWICZ
(*Murmurs*)

She's right, Colonel.

COLONEL
(*Turns on him. Grabs him by collar*)

I am your superior officer. When war is over and Poland triumphant—I court-martial you!

SZABUNIEWICZ
(*Terrified*)

Forgive me. Forgive me.

COLONEL

I forgive, but I do not forget. Get the pistols! (SZABUNIEWICZ *goes to car, gets pistols.* COLONEL *confronts* JACOBOWSKY) Jacobowsky, between us stands woman. Marianne—please go to the car. (*She stands silent, held as if in a spell.*)

JACOBOWSKY
(*With sudden determination—suddenly carried away*)

And what if I kill you! Why not? In my veins flows the blood of great fighters—David, Saul . . . And the truth is—yes—the truth is you are right, Colonel. I do love her! I am in love with her. I am happy to say the words for once. I am happy to hear the words for once. I love her! I love her! I love her! Pistols! (*He takes pistol from* SZABUNIEWICZ. *To* MARIANNE) Marianne, will you forgive me if I kill him? (*Deflated suddenly, back to grim reality*) I still couldn't drive the car.

MARIANNE
(Her thoughts expressing themselves aloud)
In the middle of the great war—this little war. What hope?
(SZABUNIEWICZ *helps* COLONEL *take off his coat. The*
COLONEL *rolls up his sleeves, preparing for the fight.*)

JACOBOWSKY
Before we begin—Szabuniewicz is your second—who is mine?

MARIANNE
(Involuntarily)
I am!

JACOBOWSKY
*(With a keen look at her, tapping the pistol to indicate
his stratagem)*
Then I must survive! (*He motions* MARIANNE *to get in front
of him. She does so. Behind her back, he empties the gun of its
bullets. The* COLONEL's *back is to them.* SZABUNIEWICZ *is helping
him to a drink.*)

COLONEL
(Giving instructions to SZABUNIEWICZ)
Szabuniewicz, you stand there. Count ten. We take ten paces
away from each other. Give me another drink.
(SZABUNIEWICZ *complies.*)

JACOBOWSKY
(Delicately)
Colonel—don't drink so much. I don't want to fight you when
you are not at your best. You're drunk, my friend.

COLONEL
(Contemptuous)
Drunk? One bottle? Water-drinker! (*Tosses empty cup to*
SZABUNIEWICZ.)

JACOBOWSKY
Before we begin—one technicality—one little technicality.

COLONEL

What is this technicality?

JACOBOWSKY

In my knowledge of dueling—gained mainly from reading novels by Schnitzler—I have the impression that the man who is challenged, the challengee, has the choice of weapons. Correct?

COLONEL

Correct.

JACOBOWSKY

Then I pick swords.

COLONEL

Swords!

JACOBOWSKY

Swords. Sabres. Cutlasses. Anything you like.

COLONEL

(*Leans paternally on* JACOBOWSKY's *shoulder*)

My good man, I am the best swordsman in Poland. With swords I cut you to pieces. With pistols you have a chance.

JACOBOWSKY

(*Weighing his gun critically*)

I don't like this gun—it doesn't suit me.

COLONEL

Exactly same as mine.

JACOBOWSKY

Let me see. (JACOBOWSKY *takes the* COLONEL's *gun, fingers it, weighs it. His face lights up*) Ah! Much better! With this gun I feel I could work wonders!

COLONEL

Take him.

(JACOBOWSKY *gives* COLONEL *the gun that he has emptied and then goes back to* MARIANNE. *The* COLONEL *permits* SZABUNIEWICZ *to pour him another drink.*)

MARIANNE

(*Shielding* JACOBOWSKY *to give him a chance to repeat operation of emptying gun*)

I won't let you fight. I'll stand between you if you fight. Your bullets will pass through me.

(SZABUNIEWICZ *goes up center and stands commandingly, ready to umpire the duel.*)

JACOBOWSKY

(*To* MARIANNE *with bravura audacity*)

Marianne! Stand aside! (*He confronts the* COLONEL) Colonel—prepare to meet your Maker. May God have mercy on your soul! (*They turn back to back.*)

COLONEL

Ten paces.

JACOBOWSKY

(*Fiercely*)

Five paces!

COLONEL

Five paces.   Szabuniewicz!

SZABUNIEWICZ

Ready—Gentlemen.

COLONEL

Ready.

SZABUNIEWICZ

(*Counts*)

One—two—three—four . . .

(*So intent are they on the combat that before they know it the Germans are upon them: A German patrol has appeared on the highway. It is led by a* FIRST LIEUTENANT, *accompanied by a* GESTAPO MAN, *who has not yet found time during the lightning advance of the Nazis to change his tourist's garb for a uniform. He wears a green hat with*

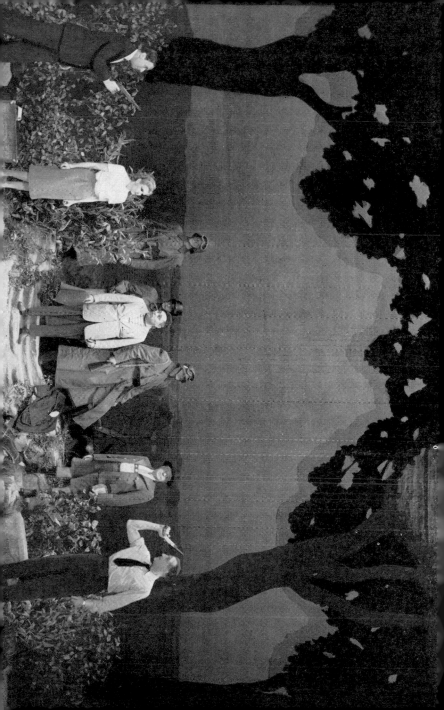

*shaving-brush, anklets, Tyrolean socks, shorts, bright yel-
low jacket. He lisps. The* LIEUTENANT *approaches the group
of fugitives, the* GESTAPO MAN *behind him.)*

GESTAPO MAN
(With his lisp)
Interethting thpectacle. *(To soldier)* Ditharm them. *(The two
soldiers collect the guns)* Highly interethting.
(Between the LIEUTENANT *and the* GESTAPO MAN *is the blis-
tering antagonism that the Regular Army feels for the
interfering "psychological experts" who have become the
Fuehrer's pets.)*

LIEUTENANT
(Short)
What's this duel about? *(*JACOBOWSKY *looks from one to the
other of the Germans and is inspired suddenly with a desperate
improvisation. In dumb-show he points to the* COLONEL, *and
makes a gesture to his forehead indicating that the* COLONEL *is
crazy)* What?

JACOBOWSKY
(Tapping his forehead)
An obsession, sir.

GESTAPO MAN
Obthethion? What thort of obthethion?

JACOBOWSKY
May I explain?

LIEUTENANT
(Pointing his gun at JACOBOWSKY)
You'd better.

JACOBOWSKY
This poor man . . . *(He points to* COLONEL.)

LIEUTENANT
Yes? *(As* JACOBOWSKY *taps his forehead)* What's he doing at
large?

JACOBOWSKY

You Germans freed him.

LIEUTENANT

What?

JACOBOWSKY

When your planes bombed the insane asylum at Nantes—by accident of course—Madame Deloupe here (*Indicates* MARIANNE) with the help of this expert (*Points to* SZABUNIEWICZ) was able to find her poor husband half-buried in a swamp.

GESTAPO MAN
(*Morbid—turns to* COLONEL)

What is your obthethion?

JACOBOWSKY

He can't speak. He believes that every man—in this instance me—has betrayed him with his wife. He insists on dueling. In the last four days, he has killed me six times. It's the only way to get him back to the insane asylum. The guns are empty as you can see.
(*The Germans open guns.* GESTAPO MAN *looks in one, the* LIEUTENANT *in the other.*)

GESTAPO MAN

Thith could only happen in Franth. Typically Frenth!

LIEUTENANT

Am I dealing with French citizens?

MARIANNE
(*Stepping forward*)

I am.

GESTAPO MAN
(*Interfering again, to the* LIEUTENANT's *annoyance*)

We have thtrict inthtructhionth to treat the populathion of the enemy countrieth with the motht polithed courtethy.

MARIANNE

And who are you, sir?

GESTAPO MAN

I am a touritht, whoth uniform ith on the way.

LIEUTENANT

(With a dirty look at him, taking over the leading role again)

You need not be alarmed, Madame. Our action is not directed at the peaceable citizens of France, but at political evil-doers and certain members of the armed forces, particularly members of the so-called Czechish and Polish armies in France. You will, therefore, kindly authenticate yourselves? *(To* JACOBOWSKY*)* You, first.

*(*JACOBOWSKY *presents his identification. The* GESTAPO MAN *snatches it out of his hand.)*

JACOBOWSKY

I am not a member of any armed forces.

GESTAPO MAN

(With contempt)

Obviouthly. *(Leafing through the papers with relish)* Jacob-owthky! Unmithtakable. Former member of the German Reich, now denaturalithed . . . *(Sharply, handing papers to the* LIEU-TENANT*)* Are you by any thanth a writer?

JACOBOWSKY

Business letters only.

GESTAPO MAN

A parathite on the body of humanity. How did you fall in with thethe people?

JACOBOWSKY

I undertook to help this lady recover her husband.

LIEUTENANT

(*To* GESTAPO MAN, *returning papers to him*)
The papers are in order.

JACOBOWSKY

(*Reaches for papers*)
This is all? I may leave?

GESTAPO MAN

No, you may not leave. I'll keep your paperth.

JACOBOWSKY

(*Pale*)
But without papers I am . . .

GESTAPO MAN

(*With a malicious grin*)
Without paperth you are exthactly what you are with paperth.
Come to thee me at headquarterth tomorrow. I may return them.
(*He folds the papers*) Nextht!

(SZABUNIEWICZ *takes passport out of his coat pocket.*)

LIEUTENANT

(*Passing* SZABUNIEWICZ' *papers to the* GESTAPO MAN)
Nationality?

SZABUNIEWICZ

Pole.

GESTAPO MAN

Aha. Pole! Bad to begin with. (*Gives passport back to* SZA-
BUNIEWICZ *after looking at it. Leafs through the pages of a black
book he has been carrying under his arm*) Thabuniewith—eth—
as in thwine! Let'th thee who we're looking for. (*Then*) Oh,
yeth, Th— (*Reading*) Thaverthky, Ludomir, Lieutenant Colonel; Thpinith, Aloith, Captain; Thikorthky, Brigadier General;
Thtjerbinthky Tadeuth, Bolethlav, Colonel, three crotheth.
Thublow, Thaul. What nameth! Thtjerbinthky, Thublow . . .

(He laughs loudly. SZABUNIEWICZ *does so too, but with a look the* GESTAPO MAN *freezes him into silence. Closes the book)* Occupathion?

SZABUNIEWICZ
(At his slyest)

Scientific, sirr. Trained foot surgeon, masseur, barber and assistant asylum attendant.

GESTAPO MAN
(Indicates JACOBOWSKY*)*

Hith athithtant?

SZABUNIEWICZ
(Spits to please the GESTAPO MAN*)*

No, sirr. My own.

GESTAPO MAN

Correct attitude!

LIEUTENANT
(To MARIANNE*)*

Madame?

MARIANNE

Madame Marianne Deloupe—by marriage.

LIEUTENANT
(Indicates COLONEL*)*

Your husband?

MARIANNE

Yes.

GESTAPO MAN

In our country which ith a virile thivilithathion we thterilithe fellowth like that.

MARIANNE

He wasn't always . . .

GESTAPO MAN

I want to thee thith Delupe'th paperth. . . .

MARIANNE

Papers! Didn't you read what happened? When I found my husband he was lying in the mud in his hospital pajamas. In the town I washed him like a baby and bought him that suit. I'm going to nurse him myself in the sanitarium at St. Jean de Luz. (*She indicates* SZABUNIEWICZ.)

SZABUNIEWICZ

(*Gravely*)

I affirm to it as an expert.

GESTAPO MAN

(*Goes to* COLONEL, *who is standing apart from all this—tauntingly*)

Well, my good man, how ith your domethtic life? Want to fight me a duel? (*He starts toward* STJERBINSKY, *who falls back step by step, actually now with the eyes of a madman. Unable to control himself he lifts his arm to strike the German. The* GESTAPO MAN *whips out a gun on him.*)

MARIANNE

(*Screaming, intervenes—to* GESTAPO MAN)

Don't speak to him! For God's sake! (*Embraces and pats the* COLONEL, *walking him away*) It's nothing, my angel. These men won't hurt you. They have your welfare at heart. I'm here with you, your Marianne. Yes, yes, I'm right here with you.

GESTAPO MAN

(*Calls* SZABUNIEWICZ)

Here—you! Can't the man thpeak?

SZABUNIEWICZ

(*His eyes screwed up solemnly*)

He don't speak in fifteen years. But he very strong. Nearly killed the head official of the asylum.

(*A pause. The* GESTAPO MAN *takes the* LIEUTENANT *aside. They whisper.*)

GESTAPO MAN

What do you think of him?

LIEUTENANT
(*Bored*)

That's your department.

GESTAPO MAN

Thomething about hith fathe that'th familiar to me. I've theen him or I've theen hith picture. I can't know till I get to head-quarterth.

LIEUTENANT

Let's take him along?

GESTAPO MAN
(*Slyly*)

Might be wither to thee where he goeth. They're ethcaping fatht—the Thechth and Poleth—from Thaint Jean de Luth. There'th a leak—a definite leak. I think I'll let thith fellow go—but on a leath. He will lead uth to the man we want.

LIEUTENANT
(*Sharp*)

Suit yourself. (*The* GESTAPO MAN *turns away, takes them all in in a slow circling look. The* LIEUTENANT *goes to* MARIANNE. *Pointedly—to* MARIANNE) Madame, you will not be annoyed further.

(GESTAPO MAN *grins at her.*)

GESTAPO MAN
(*Lewdly*)

Our Army officerth are tho thivalrouth!

LIEUTENANT
(*To* SZABUNIEWICZ)

Get this dangerous patient of yours to the nearest clinic at once!

JACOBOWSKY
(*Solemnly*)

That's the trouble. Madame wants to do that but she has no gasoline. Could you help out with a few gallons?

(LIEUTENANT *looks at* GESTAPO MAN *for permission. The* GESTAPO MAN *nods.*)

LIEUTENANT

Certainly. Sergeant . . .

SERGEANT
(*On the highway*)

Sir!

LIEUTENANT
(*Goes to* SERGEANT, *exits as he talks, followed by two soldiers*)

Get a five-gallon tin of gasoline and put it in their car. (*Disappears. We hear his voice off stage, grinding out orders.*) Right about—face! Half-right through the woods for further combing out.

(*The* GESTAPO MAN *starts to go also. As he passes him, he flips* JACOBOWSKY'S *papers in his face.*)

GESTAPO MAN
(*Tantalizing*)

I'll keep thethe for you at headquarterth. (*He goes out.*)

(*There is a silence. They all stand transfixed. For the moment they are saved; they cannot quite believe it.* SZABUNIEWICZ *runs up to the road, looking off to see whether the Germans are really gone.*)

MARIANNE
(*To* JACOBOWSKY, *in a whisper*)
Monsieur, what do you hear?

JACOBOWSKY
(*Listening intently*)
I hear the grass growing. . . .

SZABUNIEWICZ
(*In an exalted whisper*)
Saved! Saved!

MARIANNE
(*Cannot contain herself any longer. She rushes to* JACOB-
OWSKY *and kisses him on both cheeks*)
Saved!
(JACOBOWSKY *sways a bit.*)

SZABUNIEWICZ
(*Jocular*)
He faint!

MARIANNE
(*Anxious*)
Are you all right, Monsieur Jacobowsky?

JACOBOWSKY
(*Recovering*)
To escape the dragon and to be kissed by the princess—it's too
much for one day.

SZABUNIEWICZ
(*Looking off*)
Sh! Sh!!

GERMAN SOLDIER
(*Entering with tin of gasoline*)
Gasoline.

JACOBOWSKY
(*Casually*)
Put it down. Thank you. (*German obeys and exits.* JACOB-

owsky *takes charge again. To* MARIANNE) You heard what the Gestapo said. Hail and farewell!

MARIANNE

Farewell?

JACOBOWSKY

They're combing the world. Hurry before they comb you out!

MARIANNE

And leave you?

SZABUNIEWICZ

He speaks right. (*Starts gathering up luggage, trunk, shawl, etc., and starts putting them into the car.*)

MARIANNE

We can't leave you like this.

JACOBOWSKY

You must. I think it's a good idea the Colonel and I part while we're still friends!

MARIANNE

Come with us.

JACOBOWSKY

I can't. I have no papers. You go south to the sea. I go north to headquarters.

MARIANNE

What will become of you?

JACOBOWSKY

(*Minimizing the danger*)

I live on improvisation. Farewell.

MARIANNE

We'll meet again—I feel it.

JACOBOWSKY

(*Leading her to the car*)

In Existence Number Five—or Existence Number Six.

MARIANNE

Somewhere.

JACOBOWSKY

(*Gliding unconsciously into a groove of memory*)
In the cathedral of my heart a candle always will burn for you.
(*At the sound of these familiar words the* COLONEL *looks up slowly out of his morose brooding and stares at* JACOBOWSKY)
Where did I hear that?

(*By this time* MARIANNE *is in the car.* SZABUNIEWICZ *makes a second trip to the improvised picnic. He picks up various articles, food, etc., which he bundles into the shawl.*)

SZABUNIEWICZ

Everything packed. Soon begin to rain. Is necessary we go.

COLONEL

(*Goes to* JACOBOWSKY, *stiffly*)
Monsieur Jacobowsky, I thank you for saving my life. I will send to Polish Government in Exile for decoration for you.

JACOBOWSKY

(*Sees loaf of bread jutting out of* SZABUNIEWICZ's *shawl*)
May I take this loaf of bread instead?

COLONEL

Certainly, sir.

JACOBOWSKY

(*Takes loaf of bread and waves it*)
Now I am armed for the future.

(*The* COLONEL *goes to the car, sits behind the wheel, closes the door.* SZABUNIEWICZ *picks up the gasoline can and climbs over the back of the car, perching on the luggage.* MARIANNE *waves to* JACOBOWSKY *as the car starts away.*)

JACOBOWSKY

(*Waving back*)
Bon voyage!

MARIANNE

Good luck and rendezvous in Existence Five!

JACOBOWSKY

(*Waving for dear life*)

I have a memory and I have a hope. Thank you for both.

MARIANNE

Good-bye!

JACOBOWSKY

Good-bye! (JACOBOWSKY's *wave subsides. He pauses for a moment. Loneliness descends on him. Finally he pulls himself out of it and walks down slowly to where his hat and raincoat are lying at the foot of the haystack. He bends to pick up his raincoat. Underneath the raincoat he is startled to see* MARIANNE'S *hatbox. He drops the coat, picks up the hatbox, opens it, feverishly takes out* MARIANNE'S *little hat and feels inside it. The papers are there*) My God, that schlemiel has forgotten his papers! (*He picks up the hat and the papers and runs back to the road after the automobile. But it is too late. The car has disappeared. He walks slowly back, the hat and the papers in his hands. He apostrophizes the papers*) Passport to death! What a joke that I, the only son of Reba Jacobowsky, have in my hands the future of Poland! (*He puts the papers back in the hat, sighs. He brushes the hat lightly against his cheek. His face lights up. He whispers to himself*) But I'll see you again, Marianne. I'll see you again! (*Meticulously he puts the hat into the hatbox. He ties up the hatbox. He picks up his raincoat and puts it over one arm. He picks up the loaf of bread and puts it under the other. Then he manages the hatbox. He starts walking toward the road, whistling the "Toreador Song" from* Carmen. *When he reaches the road, he is assailed by the temptation to go after his papers, to go after possible safety, but it is only for a moment. He conquers it. He turns and follows down the road in the direction in which the car has disappeared.*)

Curtain

ACT THREE

ACT THREE

Scene I

Scene: *The waterfront café of Papa Clairon at St. Jean de Luz; a cramped little room feverishly lit by naked electric bulbs; at the right a bar; in the center a billiard table, small tables scattered about; in the back wall two doors inscribed in large letters, "Messieurs" and "Dames." At right a small staircase leads off stage to the street door. At left, behind the bar, a door to the private quarters of the establishment. Down right below the street door, a mechanical piano with a smoked, green-glass front that lights up and plays when a coin is put in.*

PAPA CLAIRON, *the proprietor, a gray-haired old man, is running about, serving his guests. At the bar sits the* DICE PLAYER, *a gray-clad gentleman, very nonchalant, drinking Pernods one after the other and absorbedly shooting dice against himself. At one table sits the* SILENT MAN, *his back to the audience, his head bowed. He and the* DICE PLAYER *are the only ones not in motion.*

When the curtain goes up, everybody is dancing to the music of the mechanical piano which is playing a soft, twangy, banjo-like rendition of an old waltz. Among the guests we recognize the OLD MAN *and the* LITTLE BOY *whom we have seen several times before. The* OLD MAN *is feeding the* LITTLE BOY *a sandwich.*

Down the steps from the street door comes the TRAGIC GENTLEMAN. *He has with him* SENATOR BRISSON, *a distinguished old man with beautiful white hair and a rosy complexion. The two thread their way through the dancers to the billiard table, center.*

TRAGIC GENTLEMAN
(*Observing the scene*)
Danse Macabre! In their homes they are lonely. Terror lurks

131

in closets! Here they drink. They dance. They hear the bad news. They think: "When we are together we are safe." This is an error. It only simplifies things for the Germans.

SENATOR
(*Affably*)
What happiness to meet you, old friend, after all these years!

TRAGIC GENTLEMAN
Tell me, Senator, frankly, do I look as old to you as you do to me?

SENATOR
(*Almost too sympathetic*)
You do look rather tired!

TRAGIC GENTLEMAN
I thought I would cure my heartache by walking. That was an illusion. Now my feet ache and my heart as well.

SENATOR
You used to be good at billiards. Let's have a game. It will distract you.

TRAGIC GENTLEMAN
Very well. I'll try that too.
(*They take cues, chalk them.*)

DICE PLAYER
(*At the bar*)
Cognac, please!

CLAIRON
(*Hurrying to him*)
All right. All right. I have only two hands. (*As he passes the* SENATOR *the latter questions him.*)

SENATOR
Who is that fellow at the bar?

CLAIRON
(Whispers back)

Gestapo!

SENATOR

Ah! *(He transmits the information to the* TRAGIC GENTLEMAN*)*
Gestapo!

TRAGIC GENTLEMAN

Why do they need Gestapo when we have so many traitors
of our own?

SENATOR

I beg you not to be violent against those who only are trying
to accommodate themselves to the new situation. After all we—
you and I—are intellectuals. We must be detached.

TRAGIC GENTLEMAN
(Humorously)

Of all traitors the intellectuals are always the most logical!
(The SENATOR *and the* TRAGIC GENTLEMAN *are just starting to play
when* JACOBOWSKY *hurries in. He wears his hat, overcoat and
carries* MARIANNE's *hatbox. The* TRAGIC GENTLEMAN *recognizes him
and calls over to him)* Well, well, the Santa Claus from the
establishment of Madame Bouffier! The purveyor of *marrons
glacés!* What brings you to this mouse trap?

JACOBOWSKY

The green cheese of hope.

TRAGIC GENTLEMAN

Cheese is rationed, my friend. And as for hope—it is an ex-
tinct commodity. May I introduce an old friend I just ran into?
(Introducing) Senator Brisson—Monsieur Jacobowsky. *(They
bow)* We were at the Sorbonne together. My friend is not only
a Senator—he is also an intellectual.

JACOBOWSKY

Unusual combination in any country. *(He looks around the
café.)*

SENATOR
(*Amiably*)

Not in France, sir!

TRAGIC GENTLEMAN

You are looking for someone?

JACOBOWSKY

A demented man.

TRAGIC GENTLEMAN

Take your pick.

JACOBOWSKY

A demented man and a beautiful lady.

(*Seated right at a table in the corner is the* DANCING COUPLE, *momentarily resting. They sit staring into space, not talking, rigid with liquor, stiff, ghastly, expressionless.*)

TRAGIC GENTLEMAN

There!

JACOBOWSKY

There are many varieties, you know. I once took a course in abnormal psychology. I wanted to find out how to get along with certain relatives. (*Suddenly, out of his immobile trance, the male member of the* DANCING COUPLE *leaps up, makes a threatening gesture to his companion, bangs the table fiercely, then sits down abruptly*) Very interesting. Nervous type! Spasmodic! (*He has been eyeing the* DICE PLAYER *who has started to hum*) That man at the bar, on the contrary, is not nervous at all. He is extraordinarily calm.

(*The radio breaks in—the voice of Marshal Pétain.*)

RADIO VOICE
(*With much coughing and spluttering*)

. . . And I say the nation was not equal to its task. . . .

SENATOR
(*Blissful*)

Ah, Pétain!

RADIO VOICE

Led to the abyss by political charlatans, feeble men and ideas, France resorted only hesitantly to arms. . . . But France, though prostrate, is not defeated. . . .

TRAGIC GENTLEMAN

The arch-defeatist denies defeat.

JACOBOWSKY

Who is that?

SENATOR
(*Solemnly*)

Our leader—the Marshal Pétain.

RADIO VOICE

In the architecture of the New Europe . . .

TRAGIC GENTLEMAN

Can no one silence that death rattle?

CLAIRON

I can! (*He snaps off the radio.*)

SENATOR
(*To* TRAGIC GENTLEMAN, *gently chiding*)

Be careful, my dear friend . . . It is easy to be critical when you haven't the responsibility of power. After all, this gallant old man has to lead the nation out of our democratic chaos into the New Order.

TRAGIC GENTLEMAN
(*Recognizing at once the familiar cadence of appease-
ment*)

You too!

SENATOR

(*With a side glance at the* DICE PLAYER)

Your pessimism is unjustified, my dear friend. Things will right themselves. The German spirit is practical as well as mystical. It will unify Europe.

TRAGIC GENTLEMAN

(*Aware of what the* SENATOR *is doing*)

Talk louder. Perhaps he didn't hear you.

SENATOR

My old friend, you hurt my feelings. Please believe me—this bacillus of democracy imported from England and America—this infection . . .

JACOBOWSKY

(*Interrupting*)

Excuse me, but was the French Revolution an importation?

SENATOR

May I ask, sir, are you a citizen of France?

JACOBOWSKY

Unfortunately not.

SENATOR

On what passport do you travel?

JACOBOWSKY

I had a passport leading to nowhere but even that was confiscated by the New Order. They want to unify me out of existence.

SENATOR

(*Tolerantly*)

One could scarcely expect an objective opinion from a man in your position.

JACOBOWSKY

You are right, my dear Senator. I am nobody. I am a hunted man, but in this world a hunted man has one advantage. He can never be the hunter.

TRAGIC GENTLEMAN

But you, Senator, with a little German tuition, should make an excellent hunter. You will soon be hunting Jacobowsky. Perfect sport. No poaching laws, no penalties.

SENATOR

(*To* TRAGIC GENTLEMAN)

In this great convulsion of humanity what happens to Jacobowsky is none of our business. It shouldn't concern us (*Turns to* JACOBOWSKY) if you'll pardon my saying so. . . .

(JACOBOWSKY *makes an absolving bow.*)

TRAGIC GENTLEMAN

If you'll pardon my saying so—it concerns us very much. You remember when the Hitler pestilence first broke out in Germany we all of us said, "What happens to Jacobowsky is none of our business." And when it spread from Vienna to Prague we said the same thing. "It's none of our business." But if instead we, and the British and the Americans and the Poles, had said: "It is our business—Jacobowsky is a man too. We can't allow human beings to be treated so"—in six weeks with six divisions we could have exterminated this pestilence in Germany. In other words, my dear Senator, it was we who made Hitler. We are his blitzkrieg, his victory and his world domination. Now let's go on with the game. Your shot . . .

SENATOR

(*Wounded, puts up his cue*)

No, thank you. I prefer not to. . . .

(*The* TRAGIC GENTLEMAN *takes it philosophically.* JACOBOWSKY *goes to him.*)

JACOBOWSKY

My dear friend, you remember the Polish Colonel from the establishment of Madame Bouffier?

TRAGIC GENTLEMAN

I remember him very well. And his man. Don Quixote and
Sancho Panza.

> (*At this moment, when he hears* JACOBOWSKY's *reference
> to the Polish Colonel, the* DICE PLAYER *at the bar, without
> altering his expression or his position, puts his hands in
> his pockets and takes out a pair of gray gloves and starts
> putting them on.* JACOBOWSKY *sees this.*)

JACOBOWSKY
(*Eagerly*)

Have you seen this Polish Colonel?

TRAGIC GENTLEMAN

No, I haven't.

> (JACOBOWSKY *leaves the* TRAGIC GENTLEMAN; *goes to the*
> DICE PLAYER *and starts importuning him with great
> tensity.*)

JACOBOWSKY

I just had a very interesting experience. I have been traveling
with a Polish officer.

DICE PLAYER
(*Ignores him; to* PAPA CLAIRON, *who is now behind the
bar*)

Cognac.

JACOBOWSKY
(*Insists*)

This Polish officer is an extraordinary fellow. We traveled together in a car requisitioned by the Polish Government in
Exile . . .

DICE PLAYER

Cognac.

JACOBOWSKY

Interesting variation. I was saying we traveled together but
our journey was interrupted . . . (DICE PLAYER *puts dice away*)
Who won?

DICE PLAYER

I did.

JACOBOWSKY

Congratulations! Victory over yourself! As I was saying, our journey was interrupted, but I cannot understand why the Colonel is still not here. What could have happened? Should not some effort be made? Don't you think some effort should be made?

DICE PLAYER

Excuse me. (*He walks away from the bar and goes into the Men's Room.* JACOBOWSKY *stands alone at the bar, discouraged. At this moment the* TRAGIC GENTLEMAN *has come to the table near the bar where the* SILENT MAN *is sitting. The* TRAGIC GENTLEMAN *looks at him, curious.*)

TRAGIC GENTLEMAN

My friend here is so exhausted he sleeps sitting up. (*Looks more closely*) Sleeps?

(*The* TRAGIC GENTLEMAN *steps closer to the table and shakes the sleeping man by the shoulder. The sleeping man's elbows go out from under his chin and his face slides along the table; he has been dead for some time, an empty pillbox clenched in his fist. Everyone crowds around the table. One of the patrons overturns a chair in his haste.* JACOBOWSKY *turns to the table, deeply moved.* CLAIRON *pushes his way forward.*)

CLAIRON

What's happened? He's dead. What's this? (*He takes pills from dead man's hand.*)

SENATOR

He took some pills. Montaigne says . . .

JACOBOWSKY

Regardless of what Montaigne says, when you have a bad headache you take headache pills. Poor fellow. (*He takes the pills from* PAPA CLAIRON's *hands and puts them in his pocket—almost enviously*) At any rate these pills gave him peace.

(*A slatternly, gray-haired woman pokes her head in from the street door. She shouts a warning.*)

TOWN WOMAN

They're coming in a truck. It's a raid! A raid!

TRAGIC GENTLEMAN

They're taking hostages. (*He starts to run out, stops as he sees the Nazis in the street*) Too late. They're here.

JACOBOWSKY

Excuse me, excuse me . . . (*He makes his way through the crowd and walks through the door marked "Dames."*)

LITTLE BOY
(*Cries, terrified*)

Grandpa!

OLD MAN

It's all right, Robert!

(*Down the stairs the* COMMISSAIRE SPECIALE DE POLICE, *a fat embarrassed man with a perspiring face, enters.*)

COMMISSAIRE

All right in here. This one first. (*Close behind him two French soldiers stand guard at the doors*) No resistance from anyone and please don't make a disturbance! For your own good, don't lose your heads! If your papers are in order you have nothing to fear. Come along—the quicker, the better. One after another!

(*The lisping* GESTAPO MAN *and the* LIEUTENANT *we have seen before come in with two Nazi soldiers. The* GESTAPO MAN *is now in the superb uniform of his order. He goes to the head of the billiard table and stands watching critically everything that goes on, allowing the* LIEUTENANT *to execute the details of the raid. The* DICE PLAYER *comes*

back nonchalantly from the Men's Room and walks back
to his old place at the bar, calmly removing his gray gloves
as he does so. The GESTAPO MAN *watches him carefully.*)

COMMISSAIRE

Well, what are you waiting for? Go ahead!
(*The arrests begin. Everybody is herded to the street door.*
One French soldier seizes the OLD MAN. *Another holds*
back the LITTLE BOY.)

OLD MAN

You can't take me. He has no one but me.

COMMISSAIRE
(*To the German, helplessly*)
He says he has no one but him.

LIEUTENANT

If he can prove he's clear of this dirty sabotage he can come
back to him. This dirty sabotage has got to stop and we'll stop it.
(*The* OLD MAN *is led off—the* LITTLE BOY *stands alone, his*
face in his hands. TRAGIC GENTLEMAN *goes to the* LITTLE
BOY, *holds him tenderly.*)

LITTLE BOY
(*Mumbles*)
Grandpa! Grandpa! Grandpa!

COMMISSAIRE
(*To* LITTLE BOY)
It's all right. . . . It's all right.

TRAGIC GENTLEMAN
(*Holding child*)
You swine.
(*The* TRAGIC GENTLEMAN *stares at the collaborationist* COM-
MISSAIRE, *so angry he is unable to speak. The* LIEUTENANT
moves on to the DANCING COUPLE *and orders them out.*)

LIEUTENANT

(*Pushing the* TRAGIC GENTLEMAN *up to the street door*)
You're next for a haircut. Take him. (*The* LIEUTENANT *turns to* PAPA CLAIRON, *who is back of the bar. To* COMMISSAIRE) What about this fellow?

COMMISSAIRE

I can vouch for him. Very respected innkeeper.

LIEUTENANT

Many of these respected innkeepers are hospitable to our enemies. (*Comes to* DICE PLAYER *who goes on playing without looking up*) And who is this so concentrated gambler?

COMMISSAIRE

(*Pleadingly to* DICE PLAYER)
Please don't make difficulties, Monsieur. (*Without looking up from his game, the* DICE PLAYER *puts his passport on the bar. The* COMMISSAIRE *looks at it and explains to the* LIEUTENANT) Special diplomatic passport from the Armistice Commission at Wiesbaden.

LIEUTENANT

(*Looks at passport, clicks to attention*)
Heil Hitler!

DICE PLAYER

(*Stands and salutes. Answering in a bored voice*)
Heil Hitler!
(*The* LIEUTENANT *turns from him, the* COMMISSAIRE *following deferentially at his heels. The* LIEUTENANT *turns his attention to the* SENATOR.)

LIEUTENANT

Who is this artistic creature?

SENATOR

Commissaire, you know me. You must have seen my picture in the newspapers often. I spoke here twice last year. I am a Senator of France. (*Shows card case.*)

COMMISSAIRE

He is a member of the Senate, he says.

LIEUTENANT

That Institution no longer exists.

SENATOR

But you don't understand. I am sympathetic to the New Order.
It can use me.

LIEUTENANT
(*Grins*)

Good! In the concentration camp you can begin by indoctri-
nating the other prisoners. Take him.
(*The French soldiers force him out.*)

SENATOR
(*Protesting, as he is led off*)

But I'm a Senator of France. I'm a Senator!
(*He is gone.*)

LIEUTENANT
(*Indicating the dead man*)

What's this one waiting for?

TRAGIC GENTLEMAN
(*From the street door, where the soldiers are holding him*)

Doomsday.

LIEUTENANT
(*With threatening gesture*)

What?

TRAGIC GENTLEMAN

At least he is safe from you. He is dead.
(*The soldiers take him out. The* LIEUTENANT *turns quickly
and sees that it is true; then addresses the* COMMISSAIRE.)

LIEUTENANT

Well, get along with it.
(*At this moment the* GESTAPO MAN *intervenes for the first
time. He lifts the dead man's head; lets it fall back.*)

GESTAPO MAN

Take him too. (*Delicately he wipes his hands with a silk handkerchief which he takes from his sleeve, and then puts back.*)

COMMISSAIRE

(*A little surprised*)

With the rest of them?

GESTAPO MAN

Yeth. In the truck with the retht of them. Out the back way. (*The* LIEUTENANT *waves the order. The two French soldiers carry the body out left by the bar. To* COMMISSAIRE) Take a look in the wathroomth.

(*The* COMMISSAIRE *goes into the men's washroom. The* GESTAPO MAN *is eying the* DICE PLAYER *steadily. As if unaware of this the* DICE PLAYER *crosses the room slowly and drops a coin in the piano. It starts its lugubrious strumming.*)

CLAIRON

(*To the* LITTLE BOY *who is crying and mumbling "Grandpa, grandpa"*)

Until they let your grandfather go, I'll take care of you.

COMMISSAIRE

(*Comes back from the Men's Room*)

Nobody in there. (*He goes out, following the others through the street door. Nobody is left on the stage except the* GESTAPO MAN, PAPA CLAIRON, *the* LITTLE BOY *and the* DICE PLAYER *who is at the piano. In the melee of the exit, the* GESTAPO MAN *quietly and unobserved by anyone goes out through the door above the bar. The* DICE PLAYER *stands at the piano, looking through the window above it to the street. We hear the sound of the raiders' truck as it moves down the street. When he sees that it has gone, the* DICE PLAYER *loses his nonchalance in an instant. He turns and runs across the room to the bar.* PAPA CLAIRON, *rather trembly, is standing behind it.*)

DICE PLAYER

My things, please. Steady, old boy, your hand is shaking.

CLAIRON

It's been a busy day, Monsieur.

DICE PLAYER

Where is the anxious little man that was here?

CLAIRON

(*Pointing to the Ladies' Room*)

In there.

DICE PLAYER

He may now emerge.

(PAPA CLAIRON *goes to the door of the Ladies' Room and calls out.*)

CLAIRON

All clear in there.

JACOBOWSKY

(*Emerges, hatbox still in his hand*)

But is it clear out here?

CLAIRON

How did you get in there?

JACOBOWSKY

It wasn't locked.

DICE PLAYER

(*Grimly*)

You were lucky!

JACOBOWSKY

Not lucky. Scientific. I have learned that males, even policemen, have a reluctance to investigate a place reserved for ladies. . . .

DICE PLAYER

(*Very sharp and fast*)

Now about this Colonel of yours . . .

JACOBOWSKY
(*Looks doubtfully at* CLAIRON)

Yes?

DICE PLAYER

Papa Clairon is a friend.

JACOBOWSKY

Good! One needs friends.

DICE PLAYER

What happened to your man?

JACOBOWSKY

Probably ran out of gasoline!

DICE PLAYER

Unfortunate.

JACOBOWSKY

I'm sure he'll be here any minute.

DICE PLAYER

I'm afraid I can't wait.

JACOBOWSKY
(*Imploring*)

Please.

DICE PLAYER

Impossible. Listen. If he comes—would you mind giving him a message?

JACOBOWSKY

Yes.

DICE PLAYER

The Germans are watching the waterfront. We've had to change our plans.

JACOBOWSKY
(*Nods—echoes*)

Change plans.

DICE PLAYER

The corvette won't touch here. We'll pick him up at the Mole at Hendaye.

JACOBOWSKY
(*Nods—echoes*)

Hendaye.

DICE PLAYER

That's five miles south of here.

JACOBOWSKY

I'll tell him.

DICE PLAYER

Good. (*He turns to go.*)

JACOBOWSKY
(*Calling after him*)

One second, please. On this corvette, will there possibly be a place for me?

DICE PLAYER

I'm sorry. Out of the question! (*He disappears up the stairs.*)

JACOBOWSKY
(*Stunned; his last hope gone*)

That's a man of few words.

CLAIRON

Yes.

JACOBOWSKY
(*Unable to resist speculation*)

Why is it a man like that makes you believe in him more than a talkative man?

CLAIRON

I am not a philosopher. I think I'll shut up shop. (*He goes up the stairs to the little door which is not visible to the audience and we hear the sound as he locks it. He comes back in from the stairs and shuts off the piano.*)

LITTLE BOY

Please don't lock the door.

CLAIRON

Why not?

LITTLE BOY

How will he get in?

CLAIRON

Who?

LITTLE BOY

My grandfather. I'm waiting for him.

CLAIRON

I'll find a place for you to sleep. (*He picks the* LITTLE BOY *up in his arms and starts with him across the stage to the other door.*)

JACOBOWSKY
(*Touched*)

I see you're a kind man, Papa Clairon.

(*At this moment there is sharp knocking at the street door. Terrified,* JACOBOWSKY *flies back into the Ladies' Room.* CLAIRON *stands with the* LITTLE BOY *in his arms. He doesn't know what to do. His legs wobble. From the other door the* GESTAPO MAN *comes in. He has a gun in his hand and he points it at* CLAIRON. *The knocking on the street door continues louder.*)

GESTAPO MAN

Don't bother with that. I know who they are. Come in and chat with me. (PAPA CLAIRON *puts the* LITTLE BOY *down and goes out through the door above the bar. The* GESTAPO MAN *orders the* LITTLE BOY) You open the door.

(*The* LITTLE BOY *runs up the stairs to obey. The* GESTAPO MAN *goes back through the door above the bar. For a moment the stage is deserted. Then the* LITTLE BOY *comes back, followed by* MARIANNE *and the* COLONEL. *The* COLONEL, *very tense, looks around the café.*)

COLONEL

Man with the gray gloves—I miss him!

LITTLE BOY

(*Piteously. To* MARIANNE)
Where's my grandfather?

MARIANNE

Your grandfather?

LITTLE BOY

They took my grandfather away. (*He whimpers.*)

MARIANNE

You'll find your grandfather. (*She mothers the* LITTLE BOY.)
(SZABUNIEWICZ *enters, swaggers around.*)

SZABUNIEWICZ

What kind of café is dis? Where's proprietor? I want whiskey.
(*Shouts*) Proprietor! (*Goes back of the bar.*)

COLONEL

They probably arrest him too.

SZABUNIEWICZ

(*Lording it back of the bar*)
This is the dream of my childhood—to have café like this,
all to myself. (*Holds up bottle*) Cognac, Madame?

MARIANNE

No, thank you.

COLONEL

(*In an agony of self-abnegation*)
Too late. Always too late.

MARIANNE

Courage! Maybe he will come—later.

COLONEL

First I leave behind the papers. I go back for them. Too late.
And then the car break down. I cannot start it—this cursed mechanical thing!

MARIANNE
(*To bolster him*)

The papers were in my hatbox. It's my fault as well as yours.
Anybody can make a mistake.

COLONEL

But not I!

SZABUNIEWICZ

Mistakes is human—even angels slip.

COLONEL
(*Giving himself no quarter*)

I am officer. These papers my responsibility. Everywhere I am
too late just as in Poland we are too late when Germans come.
History of my people is that we who rule them have failed them.

MARIANNE
(*Goes to him to comfort him*)

Darling.

COLONEL

No, Marianne. Please, I beg—don't pity me. I, Stjerbinsky,
have been unfaithful to my own standards—which are of the
highest. I hate myself. I despise myself. I am bitter with myself.
(*He sits encompassed in despair.*)

LITTLE BOY
(*To* MARIANNE)

Did you see my grandfather?

MARIANNE

No, but he'll be back. (*Puts boy on her lap.*)

SZABUNIEWICZ

English funny people, Colonel. Always appear unexpected. Man with gray gloves maybe any minute pop up.

COLONEL
(*Brooding*)

That little Jacobowsky—if he were here—what would he tell us to do?

MARIANNE

I wonder what's become of him?

SZABUNIEWICZ

Probably borrow from Germans passage money to America.

COLONEL
(*Borrows illumination from the vanished* JACOBOWSKY)

In every situation—no matter how dark—two possibilities.

MARIANNE
(*Laughs*)

This idea you got from Monsieur Jacobowsky!

COLONEL
(*In the excitement of this, for him, unaccustomed speculation*)

Why not!

MARIANNE
(*Delighted*)

Why not!

COLONEL
(*Threading uncertainly through the labyrinth*)

These Germans—either they find the papers or they don't find the papers.

SZABUNIEWICZ
(*Assisting*)

Right.

COLONEL

If they do not find the papers that's good. But if they do find the papers . . . (*He pauses—the thread waving perilously in the air.*)

MARIANNE
(*Exhorting him to the finish line*)

Yes, Tadeusz.

COLONEL

If they do find the papers . . .

SZABUNIEWICZ
(*Breathless*)

Yes, Colonel?

COLONEL

That's terrible. (*His flight collapses; so does he—back in his chair.*)

MARIANNE
(*Smiles*)

You don't talk quite like Monsieur Jacobowsky—not quite.

COLONEL

But I live like him—hunted! Someone knocks, I startle. Germans march across the square, I tremble. I hang on to life with one hand. I live like Jacobowsky. . . . Only he knows what to do and I don't.

(JACOBOWSKY *comes in from Ladies' Room.*)

SZABUNIEWICZ

(*Popeyed, waves hand before his eyes—he can't believe what he sees*)

I drink too much cognac. Colonel, look . . .

COLONEL

(*Turns, sees* JACOBOWSKY, *incredulous*)

It looks like Monsieur Jacobowsky.

MARIANNE
(*Runs to him*)

It is!

COLONEL

How did you get . . . ? Always you eavesdrop!

MARIANNE

(*Embracing him; she and the* COLONEL *cluster around him*)
How wonderful to see you! By this time we thought you
would be on your way to America.

JACOBOWSKY

A fifth migration is too much to expect. My bank account with
God is overdrawn already. I wanted, just for once, to see you in
this little hat. (*He produces the hatbox.*)

MARIANNE
(*Overcome*)

My hat!

COLONEL

God be praised! My papers!

JACOBOWSKY

Here. Please take them. They give me heart palpitations. (*He
hands the* COLONEL *the box. The* COLONEL *puts it on the bar.*)

MARIANNE

Monsieur Jacobowsky—I embrace you.

COLONEL
(*His arm around* JACOBOWSKY's *shoulder*)

I embrace you, too.

SZABUNIEWICZ
(*From behind the bar, quite fuddled*)

I embrace.
(*The three of them are standing close together, their arms
around each other, laughing and happy at their reunion.*)

MARIANNE

How did you get here? Oh, Monsieur Jacobowsky, we've missed you so. Haven't we, Tadeusz?

COLONEL
(*Unsure again*)

Yes and no.

JACOBOWSKY
(*To the* COLONEL)

I have a message for you, from the Messiah in the gray gloves. (*But before he can give him the message they are interrupted. The* GESTAPO MAN *has come in quietly and stands watching the three of them in their affectionate huddle.*)

GESTAPO MAN

My friendth from the road. What a happy cointhidenth! (*The three of them stand stupefied. The* LITTLE BOY *runs from his chair by the piano and stands beside* MARIANNE, *holding her hand.* MARIANNE *is the first to find voice.*)

MARIANNE

We are on our way to the Asylum.

GESTAPO MAN

Granted. But thtill a cointhidenth! (*Two German soldiers come in from the inside room and post themselves at the stairway leading to the street.* PAPA CLAIRON *comes in pushed on by the* LIEUTENANT.)

CLAIRON

What have I done? What is there against me?

GESTAPO MAN
(*Genial, walking over to the piano*)

We'll find out. (*Sits at the piano*) Oh! Ith thith piano adjuthtable?

CLAIRON

Yes, sir.

GESTAPO MAN

Adjutht it.

(LIEUTENANT *pushes* CLAIRON *over to the piano.* CLAIRON *shifts a lever on it.*)

GESTAPO MAN

(*His fingers luxuriate over the keys*)

I mith muthic tho while the Fuehrer thendth uth touring . . . (*To the* LIEUTENANT, *indicating* CLAIRON) Take him away.

(*Soldier pushes* CLAIRON *up the stairs.*)

Well, my dear Monthieur Jacobowthky, greetingth! (*He starts playing the piano, a lovely song of Schumann.*)

JACOBOWSKY

Greetings!

GESTAPO MAN

(*While he plays*)

Why didn't you come to thee me at headquarterth to get your paperth back?

JACOBOWSKY

I was delayed.

GESTAPO MAN

Mutht have been thomething very vital to thtop you getting your paperth. You mutht be aware that without your paperth you have no identity at all?

JACOBOWSKY

In my case that's an advantage.

GESTAPO MAN

(*Laughs*)

Very good. Very amuthing. (*He plays on, lost in* schwärmerei) Ithn't it exquithite? It maketh me thigh for home, for the dear German landthcape. (*Recites*)

"*Im wunderschönen Monat Mai,*
Als alle Knospen sprangen,
Da ist in meinem Herzen,
Die Liebe aufgegangen."

Ithn't that exquithite?

JACOBOWSKY

Pardon me—but those words are by Heine.

GESTAPO MAN

Of courth they are. But I am a liberal. Exthtremely liberal. (*He stops playing suddenly, his esthetic mood vanished. He gets up, walks across the room and faces* MARIANNE *and the* COLONEL, *huddled together at the foot of the bar. He confronts the* COLONEL) Well, my dumb friend, thtill jealouth?

MARIANNE

Please, sir, don't excite him.
     (*The* LIEUTENANT *goes out through the door above the bar.*)

GESTAPO MAN

Why not? Why don't you get yourthelf a man? You're young and healthy. One of my boyth would oblige you. Though our Fuehrer hath well thaid you Frenth are white niggerth, in your cathe I'd be glad to overlook that. Ath I thay, I'm a liberal . . .

COLONEL
(*Bursting out*)

This is not to endure!

GESTAPO MAN
(*Turns, facing his soldier, triumphant at having made the* COLONEL *drop his pose; throws his arms outward*)
Ah! He thpeakth!

COLONEL

Yes. I speak. (*He becomes exhilarated, demoniac, inspired. He seizes the* GESTAPO MAN *in a great embrace, lifts him from the floor and, holding him before him like a shield, backs away toward the bar. The Nazi advances, pistol pointed. The* COLONEL's *voice rings out triumphant*) Shoot! Shoot us both! I die but he dies.

JACOBOWSKY

(*Involuntary admiration, breathes out loud*)

Samson!

COLONEL

(*Inspired*)

My shield—worm for shield! This is nature's use for worms! (*To his little stupefied group*) Get behind me. (*They all get behind him. He shouts to the Nazi*) Shoot! Shoot!

(*The Nazi advances. He is covering them with his tommy gun, bewildered—doesn't know what to do.*)

GESTAPO MAN

Let me go!

COLONEL

I want to die with you. This is the embrace of death!

GESTAPO MAN

(*Struggling*)

Let me go!

COLONEL

To die like this is to live!

GESTAPO MAN

(*To Nazi soldier*)

Lower your gun—I'll let you go!

COLONEL

You are a lie and your words are a lie.

(LIEUTENANT *enters from the left—points his gun at* COLONEL. *All jockey for position.* SZABUNIEWICZ, *who is behind the* LIEUTENANT *when he comes in, knocks him down and pushes him off stage. There is a thud off stage*)

Marianne, get his gun. (*She takes the* GESTAPO MAN's *gun from his pocket*) Put it in his back. (*She does so.*)

GESTAPO MAN

(*To the remaining Nazi, who is still covering them*)
Put down your gun. *Put down your gun.*
(*German soldier puts gun on the billiard table.*)

COLONEL

Szabuniewicz! (SZABUNIEWICZ *comes back into the room*) Put
him in Ladies' Room.

SZABUNIEWICZ

(*Doing so*)
I put! Go. Go—you! (*He pushes Nazi soldier up and into the
Ladies' Room.*)

COLONEL

Lock the door.
(SZABUNIEWICZ *does so and then takes Nazi's tommy gun
from the billiard table and covers the* GESTAPO MAN *with it.
The* COLONEL *lets the* GESTAPO MAN *go and covers him too
with his gun which he has taken from* MARIANNE. *The*
GESTAPO MAN *straightens his tunic calmly and walks across
toward the piano.*)

COLONEL

(*To* MARIANNE)
Marianne, go to wait outside. Wait as if nothing is happening.
(MARIANNE *takes the* LITTLE BOY *and goes out with him.*)

GESTAPO MAN

What do you mean to do now? (*He moves up toward the
stairs.*)

COLONEL

Don't move.

GESTAPO MAN

You have the gun, and I am unarmed. Thall we negothiate?

COLONEL

Not with you.

GESTAPO MAN

I know you, Colonel Thtjerbinthky. You are a thurvival from a dead patht. Your code won't permit you to thoot an unarmed man.

COLONEL

You Nazis do it.

GESTAPO MAN

Ah! That'th different. We are not ditheathed by codeth. We have abolithed conthienth. That'th why your victorieth over uth don't latht—becauth when you win you are drugged by a thenth of guilt. Now my boyth—Wilhelm, Maxth—they don't underthtand thivalry, but they do know how to kill. (*His voice rises.*)

COLONEL

Keep your voice down.

GESTAPO MAN

All you have ith your code. If you break your code you are nothing—you are dethtroyed . . . (*As if addressing two men behind the* COLONEL) Wilhelm—Maxth—in here quick.

> (*Obeying a reflex action, feeling that they are about to be attacked from behind, the* COLONEL *and* SZABUNIEWICZ *turn to face the unseen enemy.* SZABUNIEWICZ *runs into the other room to see who is there. Immediately they turn, the* GESTAPO MAN *bolts for the door to the street. The* COLONEL *swings around just in time and shoots him. The* GESTAPO MAN *falls dead.*)

SZABUNIEWICZ

(*Comes back into the room*)

No one in there, Colonel.

COLONEL

I have broken my code and it feels wonderful.

JACOBOWSKY

Now, Colonel, we are lost.

COLONEL

(*Intoxicated with himself*)

On the contrary, this brings back the old days when I am in uniform. I am new found.

JACOBOWSKY

I think I am mislaid. I have a message for you from the Messiah in the gray gloves.

COLONEL

What did he say?

JACOBOWSKY

The corvette that takes you to England sails from Hendaye.

COLONEL

Hendaye. Good! We go! (*Picks up hatbox*) You come with us. . . .

JACOBOWSKY

No use. I asked him. He said, "Out of the question."

COLONEL

(*Completely restored to himself now; with Olympian authority*)

You come with us. From now on you take orders from me. I take you under my wing. Jacobowsky child, I adopt you! (*He goes. Swept up by the torrent,* JACOBOWSKY *is carried along.*)

Curtain

ACT THREE

Scene II

Scene: *The Mole at Hendaye, late that evening.*

A stone causeway juts out into the water, littered with barrels and boxes. On the left a few denuded, sepulchral poplars stand against the sky. On the right, MARIANNE *sits on the steps of the causeway, the* LITTLE BOY *she has picked up at* PAPA CLAIRON's *asleep in her lap. It is a dark night with drifting clouds and fitful moonlight.*

SZABUNIEWICZ *is standing guard over her.*

As the curtain rises, the silence is punctured with machine-gun shots.

SZABUNIEWICZ
(Pistol in his hand)
German everywhere. On the hunt everywhere.

MARIANNE
And the Englishman—no sign?

SZABUNIEWICZ
Nowhere.

MARIANNE
Why don't you go, Szabuniewicz? I know you're impatient. Go.

SZABUNIEWICZ
(Faintly derisive)
No. Colonel tells me to stay and guard you.

MARIANNE
I'll be all right. . . .

161

SZABUNIEWICZ

I guard! On radio I hear new edict. Because someone kill Gestapo man all aliens and Jews got to be killed on sight.

MARIANNE
(*Sighs*)

Poor Monsieur Jacobowsky!

SZABUNIEWICZ
(*Peers at her closely*)

Why you don't say poor Colonel? Colonel alien too. (*She looks at him, doesn't answer*) Don't blame you. Colonel not man he was.

MARIANNE

Why do you say that?

SZABUNIEWICZ

Begin to think—very painful. (*He makes a wry face.* MARIANNE *smiles*) You like him this way? You do this to him.

MARIANNE

Not I, Szabuniewicz.

SZABUNIEWICZ

Who then?

MARIANNE
(*Softly*)

It's being hunted. It's being helpless.
(JACOBOWSKY *comes running in. He is pretty shaky.*)

SZABUNIEWICZ

You find him? The man in the gray gloves?
(JACOBOWSKY *shakes his head; passes a hand across his forehead.*)

MARIANNE

What is it?

JACOBOWSKY

I was walking along the road. I heard the tramp of feet. A platoon of Germans.

MARIANNE

Did they see you?

JACOBOWSKY

If they saw me—I wouldn't be here. Did you hear the new edict?

SZABUNIEWICZ

I hear.

JACOBOWSKY

No more than two persons allowed together in the streets. Should they detect a group of three, the third one will be shot. I am always the third.

MARIANNE
(*Smiles at him*)

When the Colonel comes back, we'll be four. That will confuse them.

JACOBOWSKY

Where is the Colonel?

SZABUNIEWICZ
(*Taking out pistol*)

I go find him. I come back. (*He starts to go.*)

JACOBOWSKY

Wait! Have you got an extra one?

SZABUNIEWICZ

Pistol?

JACOBOWSKY

Yes. Pistol.

SZABUNIEWICZ

You want pistol?

JACOBOWSKY
(*Firmly*)

Yes.

SZABUNIEWICZ

Here. (*He gives him pistol, laughs. Takes second one from his pocket and goes.* JACOBOWSKY *pockets pistol.*)

JACOBOWSKY

They say we're adaptable. As this is an age of death from machines I must adapt myself to that also. (*Looks down at the sleeping child*) Asleep? (*Siren screams crescendo off stage.*)

MARIANNE

Fast asleep.

JACOBOWSKY

He will awake to a world without many things, including his grandfather. (JACOBOWSKY *looking off right anxiously*) The moments are passing. No sign yet of the Messiah in the gray gloves. What can have happened to him?

MARIANNE

Tadeusz will find him.

JACOBOWSKY

I'm sure he will. The Colonel's a wonderful fellow.

MARIANNE
(*Smiles*)

He will be—one day.

JACOBOWSKY
(*Kneels beside her—after a moment*)

You love the Colonel?

MARIANNE

Yes.

JACOBOWSKY

One day you will marry him?

MARIANNE

I'm not sure I'll marry him.

JACOBOWSKY
(*Probing delicately to touch his fate*)
But you'll always be in love with him? Of that you are sure?

MARIANNE
(*Looks at him, wants to tell him the complete truth, firmly*)
Yes. (*This is final.* JACOBOWSKY *receives the* coup de grace, *straightens up*) But until he learns a little of what you know—
I cannot marry him.

JACOBOWSKY
What *I* know! Useless knowledge.

MARIANNE
He must learn that the world is not made for him. He must learn what it is to suffer, to wait, to imagine, to endure. He is learning.

JACOBOWSKY
(*Taps the pistol*)
I am learning, too.

MARIANNE
The world needs you both—why can't it use you both?

JACOBOWSKY
(*His irrepressible humor bubbling out*)
Yes. Between us—we're a hero! (*They both laugh. He stops, apprehensive, looking around.*)

MARIANNE
What's the matter?

JACOBOWSKY
I was afraid the Colonel would come and find us laughing.

MARIANNE
Poor Tadeusz!

JACOBOWSKY
Still no sign of a boat! The ocean is as empty as on the third

day of creation. Marianne, I have a feeling that in this ark that
sails for England, there will be no place for me.

MARIANNE

There must be. If you stay here you will be tortured, killed.

JACOBOWSKY

Don't worry about me. I have this little box of headache pills.
. . . (*Takes box from pocket*) You can summon death at will.
Gives you a curious independence.

(*The* COLONEL *comes in.*)

MARIANNE

Tadeusz!

COLONEL

(*Smiles good-humoredly; looks at them both*)
Why are you not laughing?

JACOBOWSKY

You see, Marianne! If he finds us laughing, he objects. If he
finds us serious . . .

COLONEL

If I find you serious, that's worse. Man with gray gloves—he
has not appear?

JACOBOWSKY

Not yet.

COLONEL

Damn all to hell, where is he? Where he hiding? (*Anxiously
to* MARIANNE) You all right, Marianne?

MARIANNE

Yes, Tadeusz.

COLONEL

Button your coat, my love; the night is getting colder. (*He
draws her coat closer about her*) Where's Szabuniewicz?

MARIANNE

He went to look for you.

COLONEL

Thousand curses—always he go to look for me and I cannot find him. The time passes. This cursed boat—she sail—she sail without us. These damn Germans everywhere. (*He sits on the steps beside* MARIANNE) Just now in the road while they pass, I have to hide in a ditch, like hunted animal. I . . .

MARIANNE

(*Sees he is very taut, puts her hand on his arm*)
But now it's all right. You're here. You're safe. It's all right.

COLONEL

No. It's how I feel when I lie in ditch. I feel—I think, I think . . .

MARIANNE

What did you think?

COLONEL

(*Forcing his thoughts into the open*)
I think. Formerly other people lie in ditch. I ride by, proud. I believe it is right that they should be in ditch and right that I should ride by.

MARIANNE

(*Excited by this development*)
And now?

COLONEL

Now I know: all over the world people lie in ditch because I, aristocrat Stjerbinsky, did not give damn. Now I know what it is to be Jacobowsky.

JACOBOWSKY

(*Quizzically*)
Then I feel sorry for you!

COLONEL
(*Truculent*)

What you say?

JACOBOWSKY

You think because you've been lying in a ditch for fifteen minutes you know what it is to be me! It's not so simple. You have to lie much longer, my dear Colonel. And the difference is this: when you get up you are still Colonel Stjerbinsky. When I get up—I am still S. L. Jacobowsky. The ditch follows me.

COLONEL
(*Rises, on his high horse again, turns to* MARIANNE)

I don't know that I care to travel with this fellow!

MARIANNE
(*Chiding*)

Tadeusz!

COLONEL

Don't understand this mentality. Don't like it.

MARIANNE

You know you won't sail without him.

COLONEL
(*Sheepishly*)

Well—I want him around to dislike him. (*To* JACOBOWSKY) Jacobowsky, I warn you, our duel is only postponed.

JACOBOWSKY
(*Goes to him, smiling*)

My dear friend and opposite, our duel is for all eternity.
(SZABUNIEWICZ *comes back.*)

SZABUNIEWICZ
(*Salutes* COLONEL; *triumphant*)

I find him!

JACOBOWSKY

Ah! The Gray Messiah!

DICE PLAYER

(*Comes in. He is a different person from what we saw before; crisp, commanding*)
Colonel Stjerbinsky?
(*Both salute.*)

COLONEL

I have the documents.

DICE PLAYER

We have had to advance the time of sailing. The boat will be here in eight minutes. Ready?
(SZABUNIEWICZ *runs up on the pier left, looking for the boat.*)

COLONEL

Ready, Marianne? Ready, Jacobowsky? Ready?

DICE PLAYER
(*Dour*)

This bon-voyage party is really a charming notion, but I made an appointment with one, not with four. This is not a Cook's tour.

SZABUNIEWICZ

I don't go.

COLONEL

My man, Szabuniewicz, trustworthy fellow.

SZABUNIEWICZ
(*From the pier*)

Very confidential.

COLONEL
(*To* SZABUNIEWICZ)

In name of Polish Government I appoint you listening post.

SZABUNIEWICZ

I listen. As masseur and attendant in insane asylum, I get contact to highest political circles.

DICE PLAYER
(*Indicates* MARIANNE)

And she?

COLONEL

My wife.

DICE PLAYER

It's very difficult . . . We're full. . . .

COLONEL
(*Breaks in*)

Without my wife I don't go.

DICE PLAYER

Very well. For her I'll stretch a point. Two places.

COLONEL
(*Insists*)

Three places!

DICE PLAYER

I said two.

COLONEL

This Monsieur Jacobowsky—he goes with us.

DICE PLAYER

My congratulations. By what vessel?

COLONEL

With us on same vessel.

DICE PLAYER

Do you want me to throw my sailors overboard?

COLONEL

(*The opacity of the landlubber*)

Who cares how many people go on a boat?

DICE PLAYER

You appear to be just as you were described to me. We English are fighting for our lives. We are removing only our own subjects and fighting men, as every experienced soldier is of the utmost value to us. But we can be quite brutal when we have to. On our last trip it was necessary to drive weeping women and children off the boat. I don't care to repeat the experience.

COLONEL

Many kinds of fighting men. This Jacobowsky fight with his brain.

DICE PLAYER

Sorry. I'm not ferrying intellectuals.

COLONEL

(*Grabs him as he turns to go*)

Damn all to hell! Listen to me. He is soldier like me. For days now we are in flight. With his property and with his own life he protect the cause of my people who bring him only bad before. Two times now, by clever turn of mind he rescue my life. He rescue papers. I ask you, as officer, can I leave this man to the Boches?

DICE PLAYER

That may indeed be a problem, but it is not mine. I'm sure you'll agree.

JACOBOWSKY

Quite right.

COLONEL

Jacobowsky, you keep out of this.

JACOBOWSKY

He happens to be right.

COLONEL

God, what things a man see when he does not command. . . .

DICE PLAYER

I command them here. Take it or leave it.

COLONEL

Then you deliver the papers to Polish Government in Exile. I remain.

DICE PLAYER

Very well. Give them to me. (*He puts out his hand for the papers.*)

JACOBOWSKY
(*Intervenes*)

This fellow means business.

COLONEL

Damn all to hell I . . .

JACOBOWSKY

He's right. It will be better for all of us if I leave.

COLONEL

No—no . . .

JACOBOWSKY

Please, Colonel, forget the whole thing.
(MARIANNE *gets up, goes to* COLONEL.)

COLONEL

I do not forget. If you do not go, I do not go.

MARIANNE

(*Very tender; she is sure of him now—to the* COLONEL)

Tadeusz, I am what you said—I am your wife. In my soul and in my body. Forever. I will wait for you, Tadeusz.

COLONEL

Wait?

MARIANNE

Till you return. Take Monsieur Jacobowsky in my place. When you return, I shall be waiting.

COLONEL

Marianne, without you, I don't go.

MARIANNE

Tadeusz, listen. Here I stand at the outermost tip of France. I cannot tear myself away. Behind me I feel the country's grief —the dreadful silence of the oppressed. How can I forsake my people to go into a foreign land, even for love? Soon you'll be fighting again. Shall I sit before your picture in a hotel room in London and do nothing? I must stay here and work for my people. Tadeusz, I know you understand me.

COLONEL

For days my heart tell me this. As we get closer to the sea I feel it more and more—that you would never leave France. (*She takes his head in her hands and kisses him. In the distance from the harbor we hear a low whistle. The* DICE PLAYER *answers.*)

DICE PLAYER

(*Looking off over the water*)

Cheerio, Jim . . . Jim, right! (*To the* COLONEL) Two places. Have you decided?

MARIANNE

Yes. (*To the* COLONEL) My love will reach out to you. It will whisper to you. In the day. In the night.

COLONEL

(*Accepting the inevitable; to the* DICE PLAYER)

My wife remains in France. This gentleman goes in her place. (*At this moment we hear the music of a German fife-and-drum corps in the distance, playing the* Horst Wessel Lied.)

DICE PLAYER

That's impossible. For your wife . . .

SZABUNIEWICZ

What is that?

DICE PLAYER

The Boches are moving soldiers into the town. They are looking for us, rousing Frenchmen out of bed, taking hostages.

COLONEL

I cannot leave this man Jacobowsky here. There is no place for him any more on earth. Ten steps forward is the sea and ten steps back is death.

JACOBOWSKY

Please, Colonel, stop worrying about me. I'm used to facing death.

MARIANNE
(*To* COLONEL)

He has some sleeping pills!

COLONEL
(*To* DICE PLAYER)

You force this man to kill himself. Knowing this, I will not go. Knowing this, I cannot go.

JACOBOWSKY

Colonel, I beg you. I am not afraid to die, but I am also not afraid to live. Marianne, look, my headache pills—I throw them away. Now are you convinced?

MARIANNE

But if they catch you?
(*The music stops.*)

JACOBOWSKY

I promise you I will live as long as the circumstances permit. Colonel, you are endangering your mission. Go! (*Hands him another little box which he takes from his pocket*) And take these.

COLONEL
(*Looking at the second box*)

What are these?

JACOBOWSKY

Seasick pills. I traded them yesterday for my French grammar.

DICE PLAYER
(*Giving up*)

Very well—the second place is his!
(*We see the prow of a launch coming up alongside the pier.*)

COLONEL

His!

DICE PLAYER

Yes. I'm not convinced by your arguments, Colonel, but by his tenacity for life. Jacobowsky, England can use you in the Ministry of Propaganda.

COLONEL

You'll find him useful even on the boat!

JACOBOWSKY

I prayed for a Moses to open the Channel for me. You are Moses!

DICE PLAYER

You can come along but my name is Basil. (*He goes into the boat.*)

JACOBOWSKY

Szabuniewicz, the money owed me by the Polish Government in Exile. You got it in your head?

SZABUNIEWICZ

I got.

JACOBOWSKY

Tear it up.

SZABUNIEWICZ

Is tore.

DICE PLAYER
(*His head visible from the boat*)
All aboard. Come along, come along.

MARIANNE

Good-bye, Monsieur Jacobowsky. Thank you for giving me back the Colonel.

JACOBOWSKY

Thank you for your existence. Paris is the City of Light. You are its light. You are the light of France. (*He goes into the boat.*)

COLONEL

Well, my love . . . (*Takes* MARIANNE *in his arms.*)

MARIANNE

Between St. Cyrille and here we have gone through much.

COLONEL

It's strange, I leave you now, but for the first time I feel sure of you.

MARIANNE

Be sure.
(*They kiss.*)

DICE PLAYER

Will you kindly curtail this grand opera before the Gestapo tunes in?
(*The* COLONEL *leaves* MARIANNE *and goes to the boat. On the way he has a brief farewell with* SZABUNIEWICZ.)

COLONEL

Szabuniewicz, child! (*He kisses him on both cheeks and then goes into the boat, which moves off into the darkness.* SZABUNIE-

WICZ, *disconsolate, sits on the steps of the causeway. To cheer himself up he takes out his harmonica and starts playing it. He plays "La Marseillaise."* MARIANNE, *the* LITTLE BOY *clasped close to her, stands looking off into the darkness waving farewell.*)

MARIANNE

Come back soon. I'll be waiting.

COLONEL'S VOICE

I come back.

JACOBOWSKY'S VOICE

Madame La France. Farewell and hail.

(SZABUNIEWICZ *is giving his all on the harmonica.* MARIANNE *admonishes him gently.*)

MARIANNE

Softly, Szabuniewicz, softly. . . .

(SZABUNIEWICZ *obeys. "La Marseillaise" dims down very small but clear and defiant.* MARIANNE *holds the* LITTLE BOY *closer to her. She looks off over the water, her expression resolute, her eyes full of tears.*)

Curtain